Market Movements

The Critical Social Thought Series

Edited by Michael W. Apple,
University of Wisconsin—Madison

Market Movements

African American Involvement in School Voucher Reform

Thomas C. Pedroni

Routledge
Taylor & Francis Group
New York   London

Routledge
Taylor & Francis Group
270 Madison Avenue
New York, NY 10016

Routledge
Taylor & Francis Group
2 Park Square
Milton Park, Abingdon
Oxon OX14 4RN

© 2007 by Taylor & Francis Group, LLC
Routledge is an imprint of Taylor & Francis Group, an Informa business

Printed in the United States of America on acid-free paper
10 9 8 7 6 5 4 3 2 1

International Standard Book Number-10: 0-415-95609-9 (Softcover) 0-415-95608-0 (Hardcover)
International Standard Book Number-13: 978-0-415-95609-3 (Softcover) 978-0-415-95608-6 (Hardcover)

Library of Congress Cataloging-in-Publication Data

Pedroni, Thomas C.
   Market movements : African American involvement in school voucher reform / Thomas Pedroni.
      p. cm. -- (The critical social thought series)
   Includes bibliographical references and index.
   ISBN-13: 978-0-415-95608-6
   ISBN-13: 978-0-415-95609-3 (pbk.)
      1. School choice--United States. 2. Educational vouchers--United States. 3. Poor African Americans--Education. 4. African Americans--Education. I. Title.

LB1027.9.P44 2007
379.1'11--dc22   2007005251

Visit the Taylor & Francis Web site at
http://www.taylorandfrancis.com

and the Routledge Web site at
http://www.routledge.com

For Sally and Emma

CONTENTS

Series Editor's Introduction

Educational policies are as contentious now as they have ever been. For example, No Child Left Behind continues to roil the education waters, with some claiming it is the only way to press forward an agenda of needed accountability (Hess & Finn, 2004; Peterson & West, 2003). Others argue—justifiably in my opinion—that its policies and associated practices are destructive and have the effect of leaving many children behind (Apple, 2006; Meier & Wood, 2004; Valenzuela, 2005). At the same time, divisive proposals for increasing competition, privatization, and marketization, such as voucher plans, are pushed forward with renewed vigor.

This combination of stronger central control and increased competition is what I and others have called "conservative modernization," a series of policies that will supposedly bring about a movement toward both higher test scores and more choice that its advocates claim will benefit everyone. In the rhetoric of conservative modernization's proponents, those schools in poor urban areas will see the most benefit. Unfortunately, the weaknesses in the arguments and in the realities that actually get produced when this combination of policies gets instituted are more than a little evident, not only in the United States, but in many other nations as well (Apple, 2006).

The fact that most of the genesis of voucher plans lies in the soil of conservative foundations and movements should make us very cautious. After all, some of these very foundations also provided much of the monetary support for such volumes as Herrnstein and Murray's lamentable book, *The Bell Curve* (1994). Shouldn't the support of such books make it almost impossible for, say, African Americans to be brought under the umbrella of conservative movements and their educational agendas? For a good deal of the African American community(ies) this is indeed an impossibility. Yet, a growing segment of black activists has found something of value in voucher plans and similar proposals. Does this mean that such groups are now "conservative," are simply representatives of the relatively small but publicly powerful black conservative movement and its spokespersons who are so often found in the media and criticized so well by Dillard and others (see Dillard, 2001). Indeed, Dillard states that white conservatives often gain legitimacy for their positions by sponsoring "minority" voices who can "say the unsayable," who will say things that if said by white conservatives would be seen as objectionable or even racist.

There is no doubt that neoliberals and neoconservatives have worked very hard to bring segments of "minority" communities under their umbrella. And as I noted above, there can be no doubt that in places such as Washington, D.C., Milwaukee, and elsewhere, they seem to have garnered some support for policies such as vouchers. This is where *Market Movements* enters, and it is what makes it such an important book. Pedroni breaks new ground in a number of ways. First, he rejects the idea that members of oppressed groups who may partially agree with policies such as voucher plans are duped and are somehow puppets whose strings are pulled by white conservatives. He shows how African American activists strategically employ voucher plans to gain power in very difficult situations. Pedroni is not a romantic about this. He clearly doesn't agree that voucher plans or other parts of the neoliberal and neoconservative agendas in the long run are anything like a serious solution to the crisis in urban schools. His argument is not a defense of markets. Instead he wants us to see the realities that African American activists constantly face and to illuminate their creative attempts at getting what they feel is necessary for their children in a time when the Right seems to control much of the playing field of educational policy. Thus, he is both supportive and critical at the same time. And because of this, he gives us a considerably more nuanced picture of the realities surrounding the politics of urban education than is usually available.

Second, Pedroni provides us with new conceptual and political resources for understanding how real people understand their options, how ideologies have complicated meanings in practice, and how struggles for a responsive education can have multiple effects, some of which may be good in the short term but very worrisome in the long term. In the process, this book creatively extends previous analyses of the causes and effects of conservative forces in education. I personally have learned a good deal about the strengths and limits of my own critical analyses of conservative theories and politics from Pedroni's criticism and extension of the ideas I developed in *Cultural Politics and Education* (Apple, 1996) and *Educating the "Right" Way* (Apple, 2006). I am certain that you will experience some of the same feelings as you read the volume as well.

Of course, we know that there are powerful and workable alternatives both to the models of tight control and marketization espoused by conservatives and to the often distressing conditions we see in urban schools today (see, e.g., Apple and Beane, 2007; Apple and Buras, 2006). And these alternatives need to be much more widely known than they currently are. However, in the meantime, we do act on a terrain dominated by neoliberal and neoconservative tendencies. As a well-known political saying puts it—people make their own histories, but not under conditions of their own choosing.

Because we need to more deeply understand these conditions, *Market Movements* should be required reading for everyone who is concerned about educational reform. But its audience is deservedly wider. Those who want to also understand the complexities and contradictions of social movements inside and outside of education, those who feel that African American communities are stereotyped by the media, and those who are dismayed by the conservative transformations in education and the larger society—they too, will find much of value in Pedroni's portrayal of the ways markets are used by different groups for different purposes. There is much to ponder here.

Michael W. Apple
University of Wisconsin, Madison
John Bascom Professor of Curriculum and Instruction
and
Educational Policy Studies
University of Wisconsin, Madison

ACKNOWLEDGMENTS

Over the years this project has benefited from the insightful comments of a number of people. I wish to extend my sincere gratitude to Alvaro Hypolito, Amy Stuart Wells, Angela Valenzuela, Barry Franklin, Carl Grant, Catherine Bernard, Diana Hess, Geoff Whitty, Gloria Ladson-Billings, Grace Livingston, Howard Fuller, James Paul Gee, Joao Paraskeva, Joel Spring, Kaleem Caire, Kristen Buras, Luis Gandin, Michael Apple, Ndimande Bekisizwe, Pauline Lipman, Paulino Motter, Rene Antrop-Gonzalez, and Wayne Au. Although their thoughts have enriched my work, responsibility for any shortcomings in this volume rests solely with me.

I also want to express my deep appreciation for my community of work at Oakland University. I have truly been taken aback by the vitality, collegiality, flexibility, friendliness, and support that permeate the School of Education and Human Services and the Department of Teacher Development and Educational Studies. I learned about Oakland University at just the right time in my career; Oakland is positioned to accomplish many great things in the years to come.

I am also deeply indebted to the schools and families who took the time to share their educational perspectives and visions. Their willingness to talk with me made this book possible.

Finally, I would be remiss not to thank Michael Apple a second time. Michael has provided me with a truly inspirational example of what it means to be a deeply ethical and politically committed scholar, researcher, teacher, and friend.

1

THE MOVEMENT FINDS
THE MARKET:

EDUCATION AND THE NEW TERRAIN
OF RACIAL JUSTICE AFTER BROWN

If you're drowning and a hand is extended to you, you don't ask if the
hand is attached to a Democrat or a Republican ... From the African
American position—at the bottom, looking up—there's not much difference between the Democrats and the Republicans anyway. Whoever
is sincere about working with us, our door is open.

**Wisconsin State Representative Polly Williams, the "mother
of school choice," quoted in Carl, 1995, p. 259**

You know you've arrived in Milwaukee. Wafts of fermenting yeast, unctu-
ous and sweet, push their way through your car window as you roll along
Interstate 94's skyline of abandoned breweries and meat packaging plants.
The sites and smells conjure the eighteenth- and nineteenth-century Ger-
man and Eastern European immigrant laborers who, drawn into the cru-
cible of capital, freight yards, and water, helped build Milwaukee into a
center of Industrial Era commerce.

Turning in the direction of the near northern neighborhoods on Interstate 43, one of the first signs you see is an innocuous green metal plate
reading "America's Black Holocaust Museum, exit 73C." Beginning in the

post-Reconstruction Era, and accelerating dramatically after the Second World War, African American migration from the South provided a new infusion of inexpensive labor that fueled Milwaukee's growth into the relative urban affluence of the 1960s. As the socially mobile descendants of White immigrants fled the downtown en masse in search of a bucolic life in newly formed suburbs, they carried the wealth low-paid African Americans and other workers generated—the inheritance Milwaukee was to reap for a century of back-breaking labor: a tax base and the civic vitality that would accompany it—with them. The *Milwaukee Community Journal*, Wisconsin's largest African American independent newspaper, writes this week, "The fact is this city is dying." Its front page carries the story of a 36-year-old African American handyman—Charles Young—beaten to death by a group of at least 12 Black youths wielding shovels, baseball bats, a tree limb, and a baby stroller (Mitchell, 2002). CNN carries the story, lingering on the splatters of blood that remain on the walls and ceiling of the front porch of the Johnsons Park duplex (CNN, 2002).

I follow the signs to the Atkinson exit and turn north again on Teutonia Avenue, approaching the neighborhood of Knowledge Ventures Learning Academy, one of the five private voucher-accepting schools selected for my study of African American participation in the crafting of market-based educational reform. Where Teutonia meets Hampton Avenue, I turn westward. In plain view on my left, the "brownfield" once known as the Milwaukee Lead Works sits abandoned by the tracks of the old Milwaukee Road. A recent report by the City of Milwaukee Health Department found that 38% to 56% of children tested at clinics serving inner city populations had significantly elevated levels of lead (City of Milwaukee Health Department, 2000). I wonder to myself if this site bears any relation to the severe mental impairments, health complications, and behavioral problems that are lead's legacy in cities like Milwaukee.

But lead is not Milwaukee's only or most significant legacy. According to an assessment of housing patterns by the U.S. Census Bureau in 2000, Milwaukee remains the most segregated large metropolitan area for African Americans in the United States (U.S. Census Bureau, 2000). Here division along racial lines is a hallmark of life and, significantly, its manifestations appear not just in housing patterns. Milwaukee's color line cuts at least as deeply into children's experiences of schooling, where the city also places at the very top in disparity in graduation rates between Blacks and Whites (Greene, 2001).

A 1998 Brookings Institution report details the persistence of achievement gaps along the color line in the United States. According to the report, "Twelfth grade black students are performing at the level of white eighth graders. These students are about to graduate, yet they lag four or more years behind in ... reading, math, science, writing, history, and geography" (Stedman, 1998, pp. 72–73). Furthermore, "racial gaps in achievement in most subjects and ages are as large or larger than they were in the late 1980s" (Stedman, 1998, p. 73). The author reaches what he calls a distressing but unavoidable conclusion: "A generation has passed and the achievement of educational equality remains an elusive dream. Schools and society remain divided into two different worlds, one black and one white, separate and unequal" (Stedman, 1998, pp. 73, 76).

Educational Markets and the New "Common Sense"

Although crisis conditions in education for African American youth have not abated significantly, the last 30 years have also witnessed a profound shift in the direction of educational reform in American society. Proposals for addressing the perceived crisis in urban public education have increasingly included calls for the injection of market mechanisms such as private school voucher options and expansive performance-based accountability measures into the sphere of public education. Whereas 30 years ago reform strategies such as vouchers received little serious consideration outside the treatises of ultraconservative think-tanks, today these appear as central elements of a new "common sense" concerning what struggling public schools really need.

Given their origination on the far right of American politics, one still might not anticipate the positive reception of reforms such as vouchers among a significant number of urban African American families and community leaders. After all, the far-Right foundations and think-tanks that have been most vocal and generous in their support of market-oriented educational reforms, such as the Bradley Foundation and the Manhattan Institute, have also been the most ardent ideological and financial backers of treatises such as *The Bell Curve: Intelligence and Class Structure in American Life* (Herrnstein & Murray, 1994), which purported to marshal scientific evidence proving the inherent intellectual inferiority of African Americans and Latinos. Although one would not likely predict the institutions most closely associated with this work to find significant common cause with large numbers of low-income families of color in American cities, in the case of school vouchers, this is precisely what has happened.

What should we make of the pivotal role that urban families and community leaders of color have played in movements for vouchers in Milwaukee, Cleveland, Washington, D.C., and elsewhere? Are African American voucher supporters the newest devotees of educational privatization and free market fundamentalism? Are they simply being fooled into supporting the agenda of some of the least progressive forces in American society? And how do they believe vouchers might help them to bring their educational vision into fruition, and what exactly constitutes that vision? What are the precise points of confluence and the points of departure between the agendas of the American right and Black voucher supporters, and what are the progressive moments of Black voucher advocacy? What dangers and exclusions might such advocacy ultimately promote? Finally, what, if anything, might those who defend public schools and the public sector as vital components of social democracy learn from listening to urban voucher parents?

This volume argues that low-income families of color become allied with the otherwise conservative educational movement for vouchers as a result of the legitimate grievances they possess concerning the poor quality of education available to African American children through state-controlled urban public schools. This movement to vouchers, like other historical struggles for quality education in which communities of color have engaged, is a product of parents' agency on a social and educational terrain over which they have had little control. I argue that African American investment in vouchers is a momentary strategy chosen in the context of a largely correct reading of the powerful political and educational dynamics currently driving educational reform in the United States. Such support is therefore not indicative of a primary commitment to educational free markets as a solution to social ills, nor is it, for the most part, a rejection of a critical and progressive vision of educational reform.

The Market Bus to the Promised Land?

Any investigation of African American participation in voucher reform must radiate from an honest appraisal of the contemporary and historical conditions that have characterized African Americans' experiences of schooling in the urban centers of the United States. That this is a point of departure for African American voucher activists in places like Milwaukee is evident in the work of one of the movement's founders and leaders, Howard Fuller, who has located the roots of minority support for vouchers and market-based educational reform in previous historical struggles for educational equality (1985). For Fuller, such voucher support is a response to the failure of desegregation efforts to secure minority access to quality education and educational self-determination. Therefore, Fuller and other Black leaders in Milwaukee (e.g., Holt, 2000) have argued, school vouchers are a key component of a new Black agenda.

The fieldwork and analysis underlying this volume were designed to assist us in understanding the ways in which conservative educational reforms, such as vouchers, succeed by appealing to and connecting with the everyday needs and concerns of people who would not normally conceive of themselves as conservative educational activists. In centering the ethnographic work on African American parents who used vouchers, my goal was to answer such questions as: How do parents' and guardians' narratives concerning their support of and participation in vouchers coincide with and differ from the educational and political ideologies of their more conservative voucher allies? How do such families act within, subvert, or reject efforts by the Right and by the public school "establishment" to frame and make sense of their actions?

To answer such questions I engaged in ethnographic work in and around five schools participating in the Milwaukee Parental Choice (publicly funded voucher) Program (MPCP). I selected for a series of ethnographic interviews sets of African American families from each voucher school who were in what might be thought of as an "in between" moment between a previously attended school—quite often a public school—and a school participating in the voucher program. My purpose in speaking with such families was to discern the push and pull factors that guided them in rejecting other school options and choosing the particular voucher school at which their children were now enrolled. The first (the push factors) would be ones with which most educators would presumably be sympathetic—distressed conditions in urban schools, both materially and in terms of the negative racial perceptions that many educational professionals brought into school with them. An analysis of the second set of factors (the pull factors) illustrates how parents and families envisioned private voucher schools as offering something different from those they rejected.

Theoretical Orientation of the Volume

The approach outlined above enables a sharpened focus upon a process that Michael W. Apple and other critical theorists have called "identity formation" (e.g., Apple, 1996; Apple & Oliver, 2003; Hall & Du Gay, 1996). Identity formation occurs in the process of advocating for and utilizing vouchers as Black educational activists, low-income families, and their more conservative allies suture their interests together within tensely constructed and maintained alliances.

In the early years of Milwaukee's voucher program, for example, Black families were positioned in particular ways by both the Milwaukee Public Schools system and the alliance promoting the new voucher program. Teachers, administrators, and other school professionals affiliated with the public schools commonly understood and perceived Black families in the district as deficient in a number of ways—culturally, biologically, or racially. Black families fleeing public schools and embracing the newly forming voucher system frequently cited instances in which public school failure was blamed on the supposedly culturally rooted unruly behavior of students of color. Similarly, families complained about the regularity with which their children were abandoned to special education programs and "alternative" schools after being marked with disability labels (Corporation for Educational Radio and Television, 1993).

Although administrators, teachers, and others associated with the participating voucher schools were certainly not immune to such racialized ways of understanding African American students, school marketization efforts in Milwaukee also offered more dignified ways of understanding and appealing to disaffected Black parents and guardians, perhaps most significantly by framing them as *rational consumers*. Market-oriented voucher advocates first positioned parents and guardians as ideal consumers whose sole constraint—at least until the inception of the voucher program—consisted of artificially limited choice within what they understood as an educational marketplace. With a voucher in hand, disenfranchised parents and guardians could be seen, heard, and understood, and, perhaps most importantly, could act as consumers in ways that were often simply not possible within the everyday life of the urban public schools.

An analysis of families' processes of identify formation as they are courted by the voucher program allows for a micro-level examination of the tactical choices groups of parents and guardians make in negotiating their sets of perceived educational options on a terrain that is not largely of their own choosing. Rather than focusing only on the structural dynamics around educational marketization, which will likely further marginalize low-income urban communities of color (e.g., Lauder & Hughes, 1999; Whitty,

Power, and Halpin, 1998), such an approach takes seriously the everyday dilemmas, consciousness, and agency of voucher families as they attempt to negotiate educational structures that, intentionally or functionally, have not been designed with their best interests in mind (Apple, 1996).

Thus, seen from "below," from the vantage point of poor and working-class families of color, free market educational reforms seem to open a space to Black parents and guardians in interesting and contradictory ways. As this volume will show, many voucher families and community leaders who defend vouchers have turned to such reform not as atomized consumers within an educational free market, nor as parents who believe, as social conservatives have asserted, that private schools will deliver to their children the values that they have somehow not been taught at home. Rather, rightly or wrongly, voucher families have asserted the opposite—that vouchers represent, at least potentially, the opportunity to finally "work the system" in ways that will allow social movements and the communities to which they are connected, which have long struggled for access to quality education and educational self-determination, to realize some of these things.

The Historical Struggle for Quality Education for Communities of Color

In fact, Milwaukee's communities of color have engaged in a long history of struggle for equal access to a variety of public goods and services, and movements to secure quality education for their children have been primary among these. The move toward support of vouchers has come only after a very long history of struggle for greater responsiveness from the Milwaukee Public Schools system (Rury & Cassell, 1993).

Beginning in the Civil Rights era, African Americans in Milwaukee participated in extensive direct and legal action to bring about the desegregation of their school district. Prior to a 1979 consent decree mandating desegregation, Milwaukee's history of segregation included a very elaborate and intentional system of unequal partitioning of resources, teachers, and students between predominantly White and predominantly Black schools in the urban core. The essential priority of this system was to maximize educational quality for students of European American descent (Carl, 1995, p. 176; Fuller, 1985).

Predominantly Black schools, even in times of exceptional overcrowding, were called upon to take responsibility for new Black students, even when predominantly White schools in the area were noticeably undersubscribed. In the most extreme cases, a system of "intact busing" was devised, in which whole classrooms of Black students from over-crowded "Black" schools were transported by bus to undersubscribed "White" schools so that they might utilize separate classroom space there. The students of "intact busing" would report in the morning to their "home" school, board the bus for the predominantly White school, and return to their "home" school for lunch (at least until 1964) and again at the end of the school day (Carl, 1995, pp. 177–178).

Desegregation sought to end practices such as intact busing and sought to bring about a redistribution of educational resources that would guar-antee access to quality education for all students regardless of race. Yet the legacy of desegregation in Milwaukee is also a highly tainted one, as many studies have revealed (e.g., Dougherty, 2004; Fuller, 1985). In the hands of White politicians and school officials, the primary aim of Milwaukee's desegregation efforts eroded from guaranteeing educational opportunity to African American students into a superficial compliance with the desegre-gation decree, one that actually maximized the benefits of the desegregation system for White students. Funding formulas rewarded White schools both in the city and in the suburbs for taking on Black students, who typically took long bus rides to school only to be separated from White students through systems of tracking. At the same time, public historically Black neighborhood schools in the inner city were closed down in order to make way for specialty magnet schools (Metz, 2003) which, although public in name, engaged in admissions practices that made them into overwhelmingly White institutions. Tellingly, although desegregation meant the busing of some Black children into predominantly White schools in predominantly White neighborhoods, and the busing of White students to newly formed magnet schools from which neighborhood Black children were largely excluded, it never involved the busing of White students into predominantly Black schools in the inner city (Dougherty, 2004; Fuller, 1985).

Rather, Milwaukee's "forced busing" program for students of color, as many African Americans have called it, resulted in a tremendously costly and baroque transportation system. In perhaps the most extreme example, Black children from what was previously a single neighborhood school's catchment area were bused to 97 separate schools throughout the city of Milwaukee (Fuller, 1985).

Not only has this program been criticized for its tremendous inef-ficiency in utilizing educational resources for educational benefits, but it has also been decried for the enormously destructive effects it has had on Black students, their families, and the Black community in general (Fuller, 1985). First, Black students, unlike most of their White counterparts, endured long bus rides twice a day to and from their home neighborhoods, sometimes as long as an hour or more each way. Busing also made involvement in their children's schools an insurmountable challenge for many Black parents and families, as visiting the school their children attended now required a substantial journey across town into an unfamiliar and oftentimes unwelcoming neighborhood. This proved to be particularly difficult for African American households in which no one owned a car, and in which all adults worked away from home.

The failure of desegregation as it was actually carried out in Milwaukee to adequately address issues of educational quality for Black students, coupled with the closing of many predominantly African American neighborhood schools, has historically resulted in the creation of a movement for schools controlled by Milwaukee's communities of color. The decade after the Civil Rights era saw the birth of a number of Black-controlled independent private schools (many of which still exist today) that have historically sought public funding (Carl, 1995, pp. 248–249). Beginning in the mid 1980s many African American community leaders participated in a narrowly defeated effort to create a predominantly Black public school system out of the set of remaining public schools around North Division High School on Milwaukee's north side (Carl, 1995, pp. 240–243).

Coupled with the reality of a political climate of insurgent conservatism in Wisconsin, as well as a relative increase in Black political representation in Milwaukee, the continued frustration of communities of color with what they saw as the public school system's intransigence paved the way for Milwaukee in the late 1980s to become, with the critical assistance of conservative grant-makers such as the Bradley Foundation, the staging ground for the first modern-day voucher experiment in a large urban area in the United States (Carl, 1995, pp. 255–295).

It is within this post-*Brown* context of persistent and grave educational inequality that African American investment in voucher programs should be read.

Parameters of a "Targeted" School Voucher Program

Debate regarding the efficacy of vouchers for urban low-income communities too often proceeds from an overly abstracted conception of how voucher

systems actually work. Such discourse fails to root itself in a concrete understanding of the dimensions of actually existing voucher programs, such as
the one in Milwaukee. Although it is important to engage with abstracted
models of voucher systems, as these represent directions in which actually existing programs might be taken, an examination of the participation of poor and working-class families and community leaders of color in
voucher movements needs to ground itself in an accurate understanding of
how voucher programs function "on the ground." Therefore, I turn now to a
description of the various parameters of Milwaukee's voucher program.

Although the MPCP, at the time it was inaugurated in 1990, included
only 7 participating schools and 341 children (Wisconsin Department of
Public Instruction, 1998), the program has grown considerably over its
history, both in terms of the numbers of participating students and schools
and in terms of the expanding legal parameters of the program.

During 2002–2003, the school year in which most field research for
this study was conducted, enrollment in the program was 11,624 students
in 103 participating schools (Wisconsin Department of Public Instruction, 2002a). Of these students, 65% had participated in the program the
previous academic year, and 20% were students who had transferred in
from the Milwaukee Public School system. Twelve percent of participants
during the 2002–2003 school year had not been enrolled in school anywhere the previous year (and presumably entered the program at the pre-
kindergarten or kindergarten level). Just over 2% were enrolled the year
before in a private school not participating in the voucher program (Wisconsin Department of Public Instruction, 2002a).

Forty-five percent of the funding for the voucher program in 2002–
2003 derived from a reduction in general state aid to the Milwaukee Public
School system, whereas 55% of funding came from state general purpose
revenue, with the amount of a voucher for that year standing at $5,783
(Wisconsin Department of Public Instruction, 2002a). Participating
MPCP schools are able to utilize the value of the voucher up to the
amount of the school's price of tuition. However, many participating
schools charge more tuition to MPCP students (usually the full amount
of the voucher) than other attending students, arguing that the tuition of
non-MPCP students at the school is partially subsidized by private and
institutional donations.

Income guidelines for family participation in the MPCP are calibrated
to 175% of Federal poverty guidelines. Thus, the income cap in 2002–2003

for a household of three was $26,140, and $31,536 for a family of four, with an income allowance of $5,396 added for each additional household member (Wisconsin Department of Public Instruction, 2002b).

In addition to the income limits, a family must live in the City of Milwaukee in order to participate in the program, and the child's enrollment status must have been one of the following in the previous year: in Milwaukee Public Schools, in the MPCP, in a private school in Milwaukee not participating in the MPCP in grade three or below, or not enrolled in any school anywhere (Wisconsin Department of Public Instruction, 2002b).

The vast majority of MPCP students are elementary students enrolled in K4–8 schools. Of 86 schools participating in the MPCP in 1998–1999, 52 served grades kindergarten to eight. Three schools enrolled only kindergarteners, whereas seven served exclusively high school students. Only 6.7% of MPCP students were enrolled in grades 9 to 12 (Public Policy Forum, 1999).

Although the proportion of MPCP students within a participating school was initially limited—to 49% of the school's enrollment in 1990, and 65% of enrollment in 1993—those limits were lifted with the passage of amendments to the program in 1995 (Witte, 2000). As of the 1998–1999 school year, seven schools had enrollments that were made up exclusively of students utilizing the MPCP (Public Policy Forum, 1999). Furthermore, 12 schools had enrollments that were more than 90% from the MPCP. Twenty-two schools had student bodies that were less than 20% MPCP, and the enrollments of the majority of the schools were less than 50% MPCP (Public Policy Forum, 1999).

The 1995 legislation also allowed religious or sectarian schools to participate in the program, although an appeals court injunction predicated on constitutional issues of separation of church and state prevented sectarian schools from accepting MPCP vouchers until 1998, when the Wisconsin Supreme Court lifted the injunction. In all, 60 religious schools joined the MPCP in 1998. The vast majority of these identify with various Christian denominations, including 41 Catholic schools and 10 Lutheran schools. Two Muslim schools and one Jewish Orthodox school also joined in 1998. Of all schools in the program, approximately 70% characterize themselves as sectarian in nature. Roughly two thirds of all MPCP students are currently at religious schools (Public Policy Forum, 1999).

Broken down by religious category, only 33% of MPCP students are at secular schools. Forty-seven percent are enrolled in Catholic schools, 9% in

Lutheran schools, 6% in other Christian denominational schools, and 1% in Christian nondenominational schools. Four percent are in non-Christian religious schools (Public Policy Forum, 1999).

Although participating schools are not allowed to discriminate against children with special needs in the admissions process, they are only required by the MPCP legislation to offer those services to students with special needs that they can provide "with minor adjustments" (Wisconsin Department of Public Instruction, 2002b). Furthermore, schools are not allowed to use the past academic or behavioral record of applicants in determining admissions. Rather, when schools become oversubscribed, they are required to select students by way of a lottery system. However, beginning in 1993, participating schools have been able to give preference to siblings of currently enrolled students (Wisconsin Department of Public Instruction, 2002b).

Finally, although participation in the MPCP was initially capped at 1% of the Milwaukee Public Schools population, the limit was increased to 15,000 students in 1995 (Witte, 2000).

Organization of this Volume

This introductory chapter has provided a brief historical, educational, and conceptual context for the volume. Specifically, in this chapter I have argued that any examination of the peculiar alliances formed around vouchers must be approached from a historical understanding of the educational conditions that many African American families continue to endure in cities like Milwaukee. As well it must be rooted conceptually in the history of struggles in which African American community leaders and families have engaged for access to high-quality education for their children.

The next chapter elaborates the theoretical foundation and conceptual agenda of the book. Specifically, it examines both the possibilities and limitations of theories of conservative formation posited by critical educational scholars, and proposes and develops modifications in theories of conservative modernization (Apple, 1996; Apple and Oliver, 2003) and processes of managerialist state formation (Clarke and Newman, 1997) that account for the kind of agency and identity formation that is present in the Milwaukee voucher context.

Chapter 3 analyzes interviews conducted by a conservative videographer with two voucher parents as part of his work to create promotional materials for foundations advocating vouchers. I assess the tactical moves in which the parents engage as they reframe his efforts to construct a neoliberal narrative explaining their voucher advocacy. The chapter, borrowing in its critique from the rich debate among generations of African Americans over nationalist versus integrationist reform strategies, theorizes the centrality of such subaltern forms of agency (Apple & Buras, 2006) to other conservative mobilizations that are fundamentally transforming and displacing the American Keynesian welfare state today.

Chapter 4 approaches the question of subaltern groups in processes of conservative modernization in a relatively macro-analytical fashion. It utilizes some of the conceptual material established in the previous chapters in order to identify the key players of the dominant alliance around educational marketization. The chapter then proceeds to an examination of tense linkages that are formed among various elements of the voucher alliance, particularly between and among African American leaders in the Black Alliance for Educational Options (BAEO) and other dominant groups. Utilizing interviews and observations of the BAEO and its leadership, the chapter assesses the nature and implications of the alliances that are made with powerful neoconservative and neoliberal educational forces.

Chapter 5 takes a more micro-analytic approach by examining the interviews and observations conducted with voucher parents and guardians, as well as school principals and teachers. This chapter focuses particularly on the narratives of parents and guardians in the interviews, as instantiations of the tense and contradictory alliances that are formed among the various tendencies within the voucher alliance. Specifically, and most crucially, this chapter attempts to discern and identify the strategies voucher parents and guardians use to creatively inhabit, resist, and subvert the ways in which they are positioned by voucher reforms and their proponents. This examination will help us answer the question of the extent to which these parents and guardians become conservative, educationally or otherwise.

The book concludes with Chapter 6, in which I provide a comprehensive analysis of the parent narratives and discuss the educational, conceptual, and political implications of this research. In the end, the purpose of this chapter and this volume will be to augment the theoretical understandings we have of the process of conservative formation in education so that working class and poor families of color, as well as other marginalized educational constituencies, can be rearticulated to ultimately more effective, meaningful, and democratic educational and social movements.

This book demonstrates that there *are* tensions between the educational visions of African American voucher supporters and those of powerful conservative educational forces who purport to be allied with them. To the extent that there are points of divergence with the American educational right, and points of convergence with American educational progressives, this book provides a hopeful message and a practical vision. It seeks to accomplish some of the critical empirical and conceptual groundwork that is necessary in order to renew the increasingly fractious relations between those social actors—teachers, communities of color, critical researchers, and labor unions—most likely to defend and expand previous social democratic victories in the United States.

The findings that this book reports and the conceptual modifications and policy implications that it suggests will help defenders of a progressive vision of public education envision strategies for reincorporating the legitimate educational concerns of voucher families into more effective educational reform in the public sector.

2

EMPOWERING PARENTS AND MARKETS:

CONSERVATIVE MODERNIZATION AND THE DECLINE OF THE WELFARE STATE

This meaning of privatization is also part of a wider agenda about the transfer of resources (via taxation policies), choices (empowering the welfare consumer) and duties (enforcing parental responsibilities) away from the state to the private realm of the family. This too cannot be understood as movement in a single direction: it is more than a shift towards expanded roles for the family and responsibilities for the state. The redrawing of the public/private distinction in the 1980s and 1990s has also produced greater state involvement in the private domain. The shift of responsibilities to families has been accompanied by the subjection of households to greater state surveillance, regulation, and intervention.

Clarke and Newman, 1997, p. 28

The choice program allows me to maintain and sustain my accountability in rearing my children and it keeps me accountable by allowing me
to make the final choice.

Julia Doyle, MPCP parent, cited on the website of Dr. Howard
Fuller's Institute for the Transformation of Learning

My interest in researching African American support for vouchers grew
in part out of my sense that the educational left was missing something
essential in its inattention to considerable African American participation
in the creation of the Milwaukee Parental Choice Program. Although
critical educational researchers had engaged in important empirical and
theoretical research demonstrating the particularly negative impact of
educational marketization on the disenfranchised (e.g., Lauder & Hughes,
1999; Whitty et al., 1998), not enough attention was being paid to the
substantial support market-based educational reforms were receiving from
marginalized communities both in the United States and elsewhere.

It was not until I encountered arguments put forth by Michael Apple
concerning the role of identity formation in conservative movement-mak-
ing that my intuitions about voucher supporters in Milwaukee began to
take a more concrete form. I began to consider how identity formation
also played a significant role in the Milwaukee voucher context, but not in
quite the ways uncovered by Apple and Oliver in their investigation of a
textbook controversy in a small western community (Apple, 1996; Apple
& Oliver, 2003). Although the conceptual tools developed in their essay
became the foundation for my ability to begin to imagine a more compel-
ling theorization of the dynamics I perceived in Milwaukee, significant
conceptual (not to mention empirical) work remained to be done. In this
chapter, then, I wish to renovate some of Apple and Oliver's arguments
concerning conservative modernization in order that they might become
more resonant with dynamics in conservative formation around vouchers
in Milwaukee.

I begin by adopting Apple and Oliver's framework in order to assess
its utility and its limitations as a theory of political formation in coming to terms with the mobilization around "parental choice" and vouchers
in Milwaukee. As I engage in this task, I will identify and problematize conceptual binaries embedded in their theorization that do not adequately account for significant dynamics in the Milwaukee struggle. I
then retheorize the pro-voucher coalition of African American political

representatives, community leaders, and poor and working-class families as representative of a "third force" in conservative formation, and assess the pivotal role played by such groups in conditional alliances enabling the success of Rightist projects in education and elsewhere. Employing the concepts of *subaltern agency* and *identity formation* in relation to the discursive constructions of African American voucher supporters, I argue in this chapter and the next that conditional alliances formed in such mobilizations are much more fleeting and ephemeral than the concept of "hegemonic alliance" (Apple, 1996; Apple & Oliver, 2003), standing in isolation, might suggest. Significantly, this leaves the door more open for rearticulating marginalized families' educational concerns to ultimately more effective, meaningful, and democratic education reform.

My first task, then, is to explicate the way in which the formation of conservative movements is theorized in Apple's work.

Political, State, and Subject Formation

In a ground-breaking essay in *Cultural Politics and Education* entitled "Becoming Right," critical educational theorists and researchers Michael Apple and Anita Oliver examine a textbook controversy in a semirural western community in order to prise open the complex and sometimes contradictory ways in which Rightist educational movements are actually formed at the level of the local and the everyday (Apple, 1996; Apple & Oliver, 2003). What they find significantly disrupts previous analyses of how the educational Right grows, which "too often assume a unitary ideo-logical movement, seeing it as a relatively uncontradictory group rather than a complex assemblage of different tendencies many of which are in a tense and unstable relationship to each other" (Apple, 1996, pp. 44–45). For Apple and Oliver, the Right is not simply an already existing "massive structuring force that is able to work its way into daily life and into our discourses in well-planned ways" (Apple, 1996, p. 44).

Apple identifies four dominant groups that together constitute a *hege-monic alliance* within the social order of the United States: neoliberals, neoconservatives, authoritarian populists, and a fraction of the new mid-dle class (Apple, 1996, p. 7). Taken together, these groups are *hegemonic* in that they are able to sustain leadership and move forward a particular agenda largely through winning consent to their social vision. Groups within the hegemonic alliance accomplish this in two ways—by compro-mising with each other over what the elements of that vision are to be, and by (re)shaping the terrain of common sense within the larger culture so that it increasingly, although never totally, resonates with their cultural messages and interpretations (Apple, 1996, p. 15). In what follows, I present these groups first in isolation from one another, as ideal types. Later I discuss in greater detail the process of *suturing* and *articulation* through which, according to Apple, this hegemonic alliance is maintained, enlarged, and contested.

Neoliberalism

Because of its association with tremendous concentrations of financial capital and its saturating presence at the points of discursive production within the social formation of the United States, neoliberalism as a discursive tendency is considered by many to be the most powerful trajectory within the process of hegemonic political formation (Apple, 2001, p. 5). Neoliberalism is a particular narrative about the relationship between the economy, the social formation, the state and its institutions, and the people that constitute all of these. Because this narrative is enacted by quite powerful groups and individuals, it has tremendous material and discursive effects, both nationally and globally (Ball, 1994; Clarke & Newman, 1997; Gee, Hull, & Lankshear, 1996; Lauder & Hughes, 1999; Whitty et al., 1998).

For neoliberals, a person is most properly understood not as a member of a community or society, but rather as a self-interested individual who, given proper conditions, makes rational choices as a "consumer" within a competitive marketplace. Under ideal conditions, not only does this atomized consumer make effective self-serving choices, but through rational consumption practices even promotes the potential for efficiency and value in the rest of the economy.

But, according to neoliberals, the rational and efficient action of the consumer is hampered by the often well-intended interventions of a regulatory state. As a result of political and popular pressure, or sometimes even out of concern for its self-preservation, the regulatory state too often takes a course of action within the economy or society that interferes with the market's ability to maximize efficiency and value for its participants. In the end, so the argument goes, these interventions harm the very individuals they were designed to protect.

The remedy is simple: other than provide macro-economic stability through "responsible" monetary policy, the state should refrain from all interference in the economy. Especially within the increasingly competitive global environment of today, the state can maximize the efficiency of the economy, and so best serve its citizens, by phasing out its superfluous interventions as well as the monopoly it retains over sectors of the economy such as education. The state can furthermore maximize its own efficiency in those minimal vestiges of the state that must be retained by implementing managerialist practices, as discussed below (Apple, 2001; Clarke & Newman, 1997).

Essentially finding everything public to be bad, and everything private to be good, neoliberal discursive practices over the last two decades have fundamentally altered common sense concerning the relationship between the individual and the state, and between the public and private spheres (Apple, 1996, 2001; Ball, 1994). In the name of efficiency and competitiveness, social welfare systems have been dismantled; prisons, public hospitals, and mass transit systems have been privatized; and the security and meaning of paid work has been fundamentally altered.

At the center of the neoliberal vision Clarke and Newman find the desire to supplant the traditional social democratic welfare state with something they call the *managerial state*. Largely in the interest of promoting "efficiency" in the relationship between the economy, the state, and the social formation, advocates of managerialism seek to fundamentally transform the modern state, which they see as an obsolete political relic hopelessly beset with bureaucratic and professional forms that are inefficient, undisciplined by market competition, impersonal, and largely self-protective (Clarke & Newman, 1997).[1]

In place of bureaucratic and professional themes (which arose historically as a response to favoritism and corruption in earlier state forms), the managerial state emphasizes the euphemisms of the corporatist Right—responsiveness to customers, competitiveness, and attention to "values." In terms of subject formation and market structure, the citizens and patients of the previous state form are recast within managerialism as "consumers," and so-called state monopolies are pushed to become market driven (Clarke & Newman, 1997).

Applying their analysis to various divisions of social welfare provision in the United Kingdom, Clarke and Newman argue that managerialism does not totally replace older forms. Rather, managerialism emerges in complex combinations with prior discourses, including those of the vestigial welfare state. Nevertheless, although it is still in a process of ascendancy, managerialism has become a globally hegemonic state form. As a result, surviving vestiges of older state forms are called upon to legitimate themselves upon the terrain of, and within the discursive parameters of, managerialist logic (Clarke & Newman, 1997).[2] Within education, managerialism and related reprivatizing discourses (Fraser, 1989) are manifested in movements to introduce market competition through voucher programs and educational tax credits, the formation of charter schools, and the disempowerment of teachers' unions (Lauder & Hughes, 1999; Wells, Lopez, Scott, & Home, 1999; Whitty et al., 1998). Such measures are held to be universally beneficial, in that they empower parents (as consumers) to make rational choices within an educational marketplace, break the "producer capture" of educational institutions by self-serving education bureaucrats and teachers' unions, and ultimately improve any remaining public educational institutions by forcing them to maximize their efficiency or go out of business (Apple, 2001; Holt, 2000).

In his appraisal of the neoliberal educational reform agenda, Michael Apple suggests a supermarket metaphor in considering the likely stratifying effects of educational marketization. As in any supermarket, the customers who shop for educational products arrive at the marketplace bearing significantly different amounts of currency. In educational markets we need to think of this capital not just as the dollars consumers possess, but also as the cultural capital represented by parents' differential ability to negotiate the best educational "deals" for their children. These educational customers will only be able to purchase the educational goods and services that their capital affords them. As Apple puts it, some will only be able to shop in the most truly post-modern fashion—by window shopping, looking though from the outside, vicariously, at the healthy and fortifying consumption patterns of the more privileged (Apple, 2001, p. 39).

It would be a tremendous mistake to see neoliberalism as simply a class form. Although education as envisioned by neoliberals is theoretically gender neutral, Madeleine Arnot has aptly demonstrated the contradictory effects of neoliberal (and neoconservative) policies on girls and women in the United Kingdom's schools, economy, and social formation (Arnot, David, & Weiner, 1999). In some ways, neoliberalism's emphasis on the rational and atomized student and worker within an economy requiring flexible, often part-time work has benefited the performance of girls and women both within schools and in the economy. At the same time, the burden of reprivatizing discourses on the home sphere has disproportionately affected women in family life, both by the recasting of responsibilities onto them, and by the heightened moral scrutiny of nontraditional family arrangements that the accompanying resurgence of "Victorian virtues" has generated (Arnot et al., pp. 83–101). Obviously, these same reprivatizing and moral dynamics have implications not just for gendered relations of power, but also for relations of power along race, sexual, and class lines. Those who are racially, sexually, and/or economically marginalized, such as the mostly African American women in this study, receive both more responsibility and more blame. Finally, Arnot's research has demonstrated how the new prominence of managerialist discourses in schools and in the workplace has favored masculinist forms (e.g., cut-throat competitiveness and radical individualism), which may ultimately benefit men while harming women (Arnot et al., p. 99).

Within the schools themselves, in the name of efficiency, administrative structures and responsibilities have been radically transformed through the introduction and dominance of managerialist discourses and post-Fordist organizational forms (Ball, 1994; Clarke & Newman, 1997; Gee et al., 1996). Furthermore, the increasing commercialization of schools—the selling of students as a captive audience to marketers—is manifested in the presence of advertising, commodity-oriented competitions, and school/business partnerships (Molnar, 1996). Additionally, the insertion of public schools into educational markets has increasingly led schools to spend scarce financial and human resources on marketing themselves to potential consumers of education—parents (Pedroni, 2004).

Finally, neoliberals have demanded that educational programs increasingly align themselves to the economy's need for "human capital." This is cast as also being in the best interest of the students, since "tomorrow's workers" need to be trained with the correct dispositions and flexible competencies to ensure the maintenance and success of both themselves and the American economy (Ball, 1994; Gee et al., 1996; Harvey, 1989).

Neoconservatism

As we saw, neoliberal interventions in education are essentially predicated around a reprivatizing state that devolves educational responsibility to individual schools and families as producers and consumers within an educational marketplace. Neoconservative elements of the hegemonic alliance, to the contrary, call for a strong state that serves as the agent and guardian of higher standards, both morally and scholastically. This is accomplished through the increased accountability imposed by high-stakes testing, the resuscitation of educational canons and traditional subject matter within a common curriculum, and the teaching through strict discipline and "character education" of the values that, according to neoconservatives, have historically provided the foundation for the nation's educational, moral, and material success (Apple 1996, 2001; Hirsch, 1996).

For neoconservatives, the supposedly decreased competitiveness of the United States within the global marketplace is in large part due to the highly compromised moral, intellectual, and vocational competence of the American people. This debased stature is ultimately the result of a series of misguided and scientifically unproven interventions by educational progressives since the 1960s. Yet, as Kristen Buras has eloquently shown in her response to neoconservative educational critic E. D. Hirsch, claims of progressive dominance of education in the United States are not supported by an examination of everyday educational practices in either schools or teacher education programs—which Buras suggests Hirsch might have realized had he actually spent some time in America's schools (Buras, 1999). Diane Ravitch's reading of the history of struggles over the American curriculum is similarly flawed. Although the history of the American curriculum has indeed been one of struggle between competing and cooperating educational factions, progressives have never been a dominant voice in education, although their presence has been significant within certain debates (Apple, 2000; Kliebard, 1987; Ravitch, 2000). Notwithstanding the paucity of progressive success in influencing the curriculum, neoconservatives seek to counter what they see as the diminished importance of the teaching of traditional subject matter (facts), the increased importance of process over product, and the balkanizing effects of radical multicultural interventions (Bennett, 1988; Glazer, 1997; Hirsch, 1996; Ravitch, 2000).

In distinction to neoliberalism, neoconservative educational and social philosophy contains within it barely masked racial, gender, class, and sexual discourses. For neoconservatives, U.S. society suffers from increased balkanization and moral compromise as a result of immigration; the spirit of meritocracy has been abandoned as a result of misguided affirmative action policies; the traditional family has been disrupted by changing gender roles, including the vacating of the sphere of the home by women entering the paid workforce; the Protestant work ethic and

American "moral fiber" have been destroyed by the breeding of govern-ment dependency through socialistic welfare programs (the nanny state); finally, the United States has witnessed the dissolution of the sexual mores that undergirded and protected "the American family." This has occurred through a surge in premarital sex and teen pregnancy, as well as increasing support and normalization of homosexuality and other "deviant" sexual practices (Bennett, 1988; Bloom, 1987; D'Souza, 1992).

Authoritarian Populism

Although neoliberal and neoconservative elements have a fairly long history in the United States at the core of conservative mobilizations in education and elsewhere (although perhaps at times with different power relative to each other), the last few decades have witnessed an increasing insurgence of populist-oriented and often religiously based social move-ments that do not sit completely comfortably within either of the previ-ously mentioned conservative camps (Apple, 1996, 2001).

For authoritarian populists, there exists a moral crisis in the United States that is largely symptomatic of the disruption of authoritarian reli-gious forms by what is termed secular humanism. To these social move-ments, the perceived economic crisis is important, but is recast largely as an effect of this displacement of God to "the back of the bus" (Reed, 1994). Among authoritarian populists, there is a strong emphasis on the need for local, and in particular parental, control of the various institu-tions of American life, especially schools. Schools are seen as a primary threat to moral family life in that they are a site for the localization of elite and suspect, foreign knowledges that directly contradict and contest the sound, moral, traditional teachings of the American Christian family; not only this, but the court-supported doctrine of *in loco parentis* means that the Christian-oriented family is in a literal holy war with the schools over the control of both the spiritual and physical lives of their children, especially given what is seen as the increasingly secular, elitist, and strange nature of contemporary curriculum and teaching practices (Apple, 2001).

This sense of holy war is instantiated in a large number of conflicts over the content and method of teaching in schools, in which parents seek to wrest control of their children's lives from recalcitrant teachers, faceless and distant educational bureaucracies, and rubber-stamp school boards (Apple, 1996; DelFattore, 1992). When their demands have become suf-ficiently politicized and insufficiently recognized by education authorities, authoritarian populist parents and other activists have frequently resorted to either complete separation from public schools, through home-schooling and the creation of Christian fundamentalist private schools, or attempts at takeovers of local school boards (Apple, 2001).

Although authoritarian populists have often found common cause with neoliberals and especially neoconservatives, there are significant tensions within the sutures that connect them to the larger conservative project. For example, the neoconservative emphasis on educational centralization and nationally imposed standards appears to directly threaten their calls for local control. Similarly, the neoliberal emphasis on the virtues of markets contradicts their sense of morality based in the family and the community, and not in the self-interested competitive individual or corporation (Apple, 2001). Their suspicion of market forms has been in evidence on a national scale in Pat Buchanan's quite public calls for economic protectionism; such economic nationalism runs directly contrary to the liturgy (but perhaps not the practice) of the free market orthodoxy (Chomsky, 1999).

Nevertheless, authoritarian populists have found common cause with neoconservatives over demands for the increased importance of conservative values and a (nostalgic and romanticized) return to traditional educational forms. Additionally, their tensions with neoliberals are superseded by the opportunities that are presented by neoliberal successes in promoting voucher programs, charter schools, and tax credits, which enable their separation from public schools, as well as the leverage they are able to bring to bear in changing public (and other) schools in the direction of their interests. Reprivatization of previously public responsibilities is, after all, precisely what authoritarian populist parents and organizations seek (Apple, 2001). Finally, authoritarian populists have found shelter beneath the "umbrella" of conservative modernization through the particular inflection that invocations of "religious freedom" have recently received. A successful "politics of recognition" (Fraser, 1989) by conservative activists has, as previously mentioned, recast Christian evangelicals and other fundamentalists as the new civil rights cause in American life (Apple, 2001; Reed, 1994).

The Professional and Managerial Fraction of the New Middle Class

Within Apple's framework, the last group comprising the conservative hegemonic alliance is a particular fraction of the professional and managerial new middle class. This fraction, the least explicitly ideological among the four, gains its social mobility by virtue of the professional expertise it is able to provide for the hegemonic alliance in matters related to educational standardization, measurement, and management (Apple, 2001).

As noted previously, neoliberals and neoconservatives keep themselves beneath the same ideological umbrella by compromising with each other over the precise nature of their articulated vision, often in quite creative ways. Within education, neoliberals and neoconservatives have sutured together their potentially irreconcilable differences over the role of the state in education through a fairly ingenious design. Neoliberals, with their desire for a weak educational state,[3] seek to devolve educational responsibility away from the state and toward individual schools so that they can compete as effectively as possible for consumers within the educational marketplace; their needs are at least partially met through the approval and realization of educational interventions promoting competition, including voucher systems, the creation of charter schools, public school choice, and the implementation of educational tax credits. Neoconservatives, on the other hand, favor the role that a strong, interventionist state can play in ensuring the standardization of a curriculum centered on the teaching of "traditional" subject matter and the values it supposedly conveys, including the literary canon; their agenda is at least partially realized through an increased emphasis on standardized national and statewide curricula, and frequent standardized testing of both students and teachers. In turn, this "recentralizing" tendency will have a salutary effect for the neoliberal educational vision, because the publication of the test scores of various competing schools in league tables will permit consumers to make "informed" choices within the educational marketplace. "Producer capture" is mitigated as schools with poor test scores realize that they must either improve the image of the product they are offering or go out of business, as savvy customers consult league tables and take their business elsewhere (Apple, 1996, 2001).

Those who comprise the fraction of the new middle class that Apple has in mind provide the technical, legal, procedural, and bureaucratic expertise to make this system of standardization and comparison possible. They bring to the process of conservative modernization their competence with supposedly neutral efficiency, measurement, and management instruments—the very instruments that will enhance the ability of schools to function as stratifying mechanisms. As those in the social formation with the most fluency in such matters, their children in some ways stand to gain the most from the increased prevalence of standardized and managerialist forms in schools, because they will have a competitive edge over their "peers" in assimilating these forms, and thus enhancing their accumulation of social and cultural capital (Apple, 1996, 2001).

Conservative Modernization as a Hegemonic Process

Until this point, my focus has been on a descriptive identification of the key elements in conservative modernization. In the following section I turn to a more comprehensive and theoretical explication of the process through which hegemonic alliances are constructed, maintained, and contested. Understanding this process will be central to comprehending the dynamic and contested nature of the alliance around vouchers in Milwaukee.

Because it is formed and sutured through compromise, the social vision of the hegemonic alliance is never unitary. Rather, as was illustrated in the previous section, it exists always in a somewhat fragile tension, fraught with contradictions that constantly threaten to undo its continued success (Apple, 1996, p. 15). As the Rightist alliance sutures over its internal contradictions and infuses the everyday discourses of American public life with its sense-making constructions, it also, at least potentially, grows.

For Apple, this hegemonic bloc is dynamic (that is, always in formation) in three important ways. First, it is dynamic temporally, in that it can and must respond to changing historical conditions, shifting alliances, the introduction of new technologies, the birth of new social movements, and larger economic trends. Second and third, this conservative modernization is dynamic spatially, discursively speaking, in both a horizontal and vertical fashion. Horizontal dynamism is present in the suturing that takes place as different dominant groups gather together in tense unity under a single "ideological umbrella" (Apple, 1996, p. 15); vertical dynamism is present as the discourses of these dominant groups act in creative ways to disarticulate prior connections and rearticulate groups of (largely ideologically unformed) people into this larger ideological movement by connecting to the real hopes, fears, and conditions of people's daily lives and by providing seemingly "sensible" explanations for the current troubles people are having (p. 45). In short, this is a process of horizontal *suturing* and vertical *articulation*.

The politically formative process of disarticulation and rearticulation does not occur, however, in a seamless manner directly governed by the dominant groups' political will. Instead, as Apple and Oliver demonstrate in their study of conservative formation in the textbook controversy mentioned earlier, "ordinary people" become articulated to larger conservative social movements through a complex series of "accidents" and interactions with the state (Apple, 1996, p. 45).

For Apple and Oliver, it is not just the hegemonic alliance and the subjectivities of those who might be articulated into it that are always in flux—the state, too, is dynamic in an analogous manner; the state "grows" in response to its interactions with assemblages of social movements that constantly seek to reshape it to their vision. Although this growth occurs through a variety of potential responses (e.g., by adopting, mediating, and/or resisting the demands of social movements), families in Apple and Oliver's study who were concerned about what they perceived as culturally unfamiliar and disturbing materials in the textbook controversy primarily encountered a defensively postured state resisting further challenges by what it impatiently concluded were the organized forces of right-wing censorship.

> Nearly every [concerned] parent ... stated that their original introduction to the textbooks began when their child came home and was made upset by a particular selection in the texts. ... [Parents] were more than a little surprised to read stories in their children's books that seemed inappropriate, and were even more surprised and dismayed by what they felt was the board's and the administration's "heavy handed" response. (Apple, 1996, p. 58)

The state as enshrined in the bureaucratic offices of the local school district responded to the concerns of ideologically relatively unformed[4] and heterogeneous groups of parents by making available to them only two subject positions through which they might be seen, heard, and understood: that of the responsible parent who supported the "professional decision-making" of school district officials and teachers regarding curriculum, and that of the irresponsible right-wing censor. Forced into the latter subject position as a result of their unmet and persistent concerns, many politically unformed parents became quite ideologically formed as they turned to right-wing national organizations for help in overcoming the intransigence of the school bureaucracy. In the process of this "accidental" and highly mediated subject formation, in which the agency of concerned parents became articulated to the agency of the broader Right, the Right grew (Apple, 1996, p. 64).

Possibilities and Limitations: The Battle
over "Parental Choice" in Milwaukee

In their study of conservative formation within a small-town textbook controversy, Apple and Oliver have clearly disrupted received and unhelpful notions of a unitary Right growing seamlessly, in isolation, and through strict intentionality. In many ways reminiscent of Apple's earlier interventions concerning reproduction in schools (Apple, 1985), the researchers have provided us with a rich account of the complex, mediated, and contradictory ways in which the hegemonic alliance actually grows through articulations with the real hopes, fears, and good sense of ordinary people rebuked by the state.

In this section I explore the ways in which this approach to conservative formation both enables and limits our understanding of another moment in which processes of conservative modernization have significantly altered public policy—the construction of the voucher alliance and the resulting voucher program in Milwaukee. After identifying and analyzing some of the possible limitations of Apple's framework, I will propose some substantive alternatives.

Jim Carl (1996), in an article entitled "Unusual Allies: Elite and Grass-roots Origins of Parental Choice in Milwaukee," adopts a theoretical framework for understanding events in Milwaukee that resonates with Apple and Oliver's own theoretical constructions. However, as we shall see, some elements of the history that Carl narrates seem to fit less comfortably within their framework.

Carl begins his analysis of factors leading to the rise of the "parental choice" debate in Milwaukee by describing the emergence nationally of a hegemonic alliance in the early 1980s, which he calls the conservative restoration (a term also used by Apple in earlier works). Within this alliance, in relation to issues of parental choice, Carl depicts the tensely intersecting agendas of two of the dominant groups delimited by Apple—neoliberals and neoconservatives. According to Carl (1996), local neoliberal education reformers, on the one hand, believed that the extension of private markets into the state's education systems would bring improvement in educational attainment as well as profitability. On the other hand, local neoconservative educational reformers privileged private schools for their supposed traditional academic curriculum, religious training, and strict discipline (p. 268). Although Apple is much less cursory in describing the complexity of these positions and interactions (Apple, 1996, pp. 27–31), the parallels are quite clear and, as will be shown below, useful for understanding certain dynamics within the Milwaukee context.

However, Carl also acknowledges that "not all proponents of vouchers in Milwaukee can be described as agents of the conservative restoration" (1996, p. 268). Rather, he outlines a "conditional alliance" between state-level neoliberal reformers and Milwaukee-based supporters of a handful of independent community schools. According to Carl,

> Five factors generated this conditional alliance: dissatisfaction among many black Milwaukeeans with a school system that failed to deliver acceptable educational outcomes for disproportionately high numbers of black students; the existence of community schools whose multicultural supporters had sought public funding for two decades; the growth of black political representation in Milwaukee during an era when government policies tilted rightward, as personified by state representative Polly Williams; the efforts of Governor Tommy Thompson's administration to craft neoliberal and neoconservative social policy; and the rise of Milwaukee's Bradley Foundation as the nation's premier conservative grantmaker. (p. 268)

In analyzing the conditional alliance that Carl describes, Apple and Oliver's model seems to offer two possible inroads for making sense of African Americans in Milwaukee who have supported publicly financed vouchers as a means of enrolling their children in Milwaukee's independent community schools. The first possibility—one Apple would presumably not endorse given his discussion of race and class as central dynamics in unequal power relations—is that we see the Milwaukee-based voucher supporters under the leadership of African American state representative Polly Williams as becoming part of an alliance of dominant groups. In such a scenario, we would read Polly Williams' group as having horizontally sutured itself together, through compromises, with neoliberals and neoconservatives, thereby sharing in the (always partial) exercise of hegemonic control over education debates in Milwaukee. The second possibility, again experimenting with Apple and Oliver's framework, is that we see Polly Williams' group as vertically articulated to right-wing movements in the manner of the ideologically relatively unformed, "ordinary people" of the textbook controversy, a possibility that Apple would presumably reject given the many decades of educational activism by African American families in Milwaukee.

Although these seem to be the two theoretical spaces conceptually available in Apple and Oliver's framework for interpreting the conditional alliance around vouchers in Milwaukee, in what follows I will show the partial inadequacy of both. In fairness, Apple and Oliver do mention that "rightist policies are often compromises both between the Right *and other groups* [italics added] and among the various tendencies within the conservative alliance" (Apple, 1996, p. 45). However, if the compromises "between the Right and other groups" are to be understood as a conceptual category outside of the two possibilities I have mentioned, Apple and Oliver have not yet adequately described or theorized this possibility.

Before analyzing the ways in which each of the two theoretical possibilities described above partially explains and partially misconstrues the reality of the conditional alliance in Milwaukee, I want to introduce a set of binaries that underlie Apple's conception of Rightist formation. Later I will problematize these in hopes of opening up a "third theoretical space" for analyzing the conditional alliance in Milwaukee, and by extension similar alliances in other settings.

At least temporarily and within the Milwaukee context, despite our contrary intuitions, Polly Williams' pro-voucher faction embodies characteristics that seem to locate it within Apple and Oliver's framework as a dominant member of the alliance. For example, Williams' explicit recognition of the limitations of historical alliances with White liberals (Carl, 1996, p. 274) clearly indicates carefully formed and sophisticated tactical ideology in response to political experience. Her often-expressed realism and lack of naiveté regarding both the political climate of the late 1980s and the self-interestedness of neoliberals willing to ally with her is further indication of this; it is also indicative of the suturing nature of her relationship with neoliberals, in which neoliberal language concerning competition and markets became fused with her own vision of community control. As Carl notes, "Unlike her New Right allies, who argued that the social safety net ought to be lowered or dismantled, Williams believed that blacks needed to take control of publicly funded programs and institutions that targeted their communities" (1996, p. 274). In short, Williams had not allowed her vision to be subsumed into that of the Right, as in the case of the concerned parents by the end of the textbook controversy; neither she nor her faction "became Right" in any way that would preserve the normal stability of that terminology.

Although Williams' faction resonates with certain characteristics of membership within an alliance of dominant groups as described by Apple and Oliver (and as depicted in the column of Scenario One in Table 2.1), it falls far short in other respects. It is very difficult to conceive of Williams' faction and its poor and working-class Latino and African American supporters as a dominant group within the political landscape of Milwaukee. The most cursory examination of social and material conditions that frame the everyday lives of low-income African American and Latino families in Milwaukee renders this a conceptual impossibility, as does the long and frustrating experience African American parents and community leaders, including Williams, have had in failing to gain greater responsiveness from the Milwaukee Public Schools bureaucracy (Carl, 1995; Fuller, 1985).

This marginalization, then, seems to point us away conceptually from locating African American supporters of vouchers in Milwaukee within the alliance of dominant groups (Scenario One in Table 2.1), and toward Scenario Two, resonant with the experiences of the ordinary, ideologically relatively unformed parents described by Apple and Oliver in the "Becoming Right" piece. Immediately we are struck by the parallel between the encounter of the concerned parents in the textbook controversy with an unresponsive state bureaucracy, on the one hand, and the experiences of Williams and her followers as they sought redress from the Milwaukee Public Schools system, on the other. Williams and her followers, clearly, were pushed toward rightist social movements because of the perceived intransigence of state actors. Furthermore, within this educational struggle, it is easy for most progressives to identify the "real hopes and fears" of Williams' faction with which we presumably are highly sympathetic. Finally, as mentioned previously, the Williams faction in the conditional alliance rests much more comfortably, relative to power, on the side of the "not-yet-dominant" in Table 2.1.

Nevertheless, as alluded to earlier, aspects of the Williams faction are more than a little incongruous with the "ordinary people" formulation of Scenario Two. To argue that her group remained ideologically largely unformed or characterized in its ideas by common sense understandings would be to deeply insult the decades of struggle around education in which groups of African Americans in Milwaukee (and elsewhere) have engaged (Carl, 1995; Fuller, 1985; Holt, 2000). Furthermore, the relationship of Williams' faction to the neoliberal groups with which she worked was not simply vertical; again, the sophisticated manner in which Williams was able to negotiate her interests with those of neoliberals demonstrates a significant degree of "horizontal" relationship between the two.

If the conditional alliance described by Carl does not fit conceptually into the two available scenarios, how then should it be theorized? And if this practical example and its theorization apply in other settings, what are the implications for our understanding of the Right's success in the present moment in other contested spheres?

Toward a "Third Space" in Conservative Formation

In the battle over publicly financed private school vouchers in Milwaukee, as I have shown, Williams' group of African American voucher supporters cannot properly be theorized as either a dominant group sutured within a hegemonic alliance or a group of ideologically relatively unformed, ordinary people articulated into the Right as a result of the state's unresponsiveness. Despite its theoretical elusiveness, Williams' faction was absolutely central both to the emergence of parental choice programs in Milwaukee, and to the claims to respectability and legitimacy that voucher programs have since attained in national and even global educational debates. Given this, a further theorization of African American supporters of vouchers in Milwaukee is crucial to the project of more fully understanding and contesting the Right's continued success in dismantling key vestiges of the American social democratic accord.

As the Milwaukee parental choice case suggests, the hegemonic alliance was not able to impose voucher programs in Milwaukee or elsewhere until the birth of a more fleeting conditional alliance, in which dominant groups were nevertheless the major, and exponentially more powerful, players. Although Carl does not "unpack" his use of the term conditional alliance as much as we might hope, his usage, especially in relation to the Milwaukee example, seems to imply an alliance that is much more fleeting and ephemeral than a stand-alone hegemonic alliance restored over 30 years, successfully suturing new compromises among its dominant members while articulating ideologically relatively unformed, ordinary people into its ranks (see Apple, 1996, p. 61; and endnote 4 for this chapter).

In theorizing the qualities of the non-dominant but ideologically more formed groups that join with dominant ones in order to build successful conditional alliances, a useful approach might be to envision the opposite poles of the qualities of Scenarios One and Two in Table 2.1 as horizons, with the parent textbook activists as described by Apple and Oliver largely

Table 2.1 The Two Scenarios (or 'Spaces') of Conservative Formation in Apple and Oliver

| | SCENARIO | |
CATEGORY	1. PART OF THE ALLIANCE OF DOMINANT GROUPS	2. ORDINARY PEOPLE WHO BECOME RIGHT
Example	Neoliberals, neoconservatives, etc.	Parents in textbook controversy
Relationship to power	Horizontal	Vertical
Connection to power	Suturing compromises	"Good sense" articulated to conservative project
Quality of ideology	Formed	Unformed
Nature of ideas	Ideology	Common sense
Relative power	Dominant	Not-yet-dominant
Character of ideas	Elements of good sense which appeal to ordinary people	Real hopes and fears to which progressives are sympathetic
Relative spatial metaphor	Above	Below
Relationship to state	Attempt to affect the direction of the state through an assemblage of social movements	Pushed toward Rightist social movements when rebuked by an unresponsive state

encapsulated within the descriptors in the column of Scenario Two. Dominant groups, such as neoliberal forces, on the other hand, would largely align with the characteristics in the column of Scenario One. Different "third space" groups with which the Right formed conditional alliances, such as pro-voucher African American families in Milwaukee, would occupy various points along each of the eight categorical horizons.

In accordance with the sketch presented earlier, African American voucher families in Milwaukee—as an example of a social force implying a third scenario, or third space tendency in conservative formation—should be located along the respective horizons in Table 2.1 as relatively *formed*, *ideological*, and *suturing* in a *horizontal* manner with dominant groups (all descriptors on the left side of the table). At the same time they remain largely *not-yet-dominant*, *pushed toward Rightist social movements by an unresponsive state*, and constituted by *real hopes and fears to which progressives can be sympathetic* (as encapsulated more within the right side of the table).

Just as we need to realize the heterogeneous qualities of groups that are sutured and articulated to the hegemonic alliance in conditional alliances, we also need to think clearly about the quality of the conservative victories implicit in such alliances. Whereas the first two scenarios of the Right's growth—through horizontal suturing and vertical articulations—represent fairly unequivocal victories for the rightist project, the third scenario involving subalternly negotiated alliances presents a more nuanced, ambiguous, and contradictory sense of victory. Is the political success of the MPCP simply a monolithic loss for those supporting radically democratic reform in education, or is it also a partial victory? More will be said about this in relation to African American tactical mobilizations for vouchers later.

Identity Formation and Subaltern Agency: A Reconceptualization

In order to develop a more nuanced conceptualization of the importance of such third space groups in conservative formation, it will be useful to further sharpen our focus upon the process of what Apple and Oliver (along with other theorists) have called "identity formation" (Apple, 1996; Apple & Oliver, 2003). To recap briefly from the previous chapter, in the voucher example identity formation occurs as various factions of the conservative alliance, African American educational activists, and low-income families in Milwaukee suture their interests together within tensely constructed and maintained alliances. In the earlier years of the MPCP, discourses circulating through the Milwaukee Public Schools system, as well as through the voucher alliance, positioned African American families and offered identities in particular ways. Primary among the subject positions in circulation among teachers, administrators, and other professionals in the Milwaukee Public Schools were those predicated on culturally based, racially based, and/or biologically based deficit models. African American families fleeing public schools and embracing the proposed voucher system frequently cited instances in which public school failure was blamed on the supposedly culturally rooted unruly behavior of students of color. Similarly, families complained about the regularity with which their children were pathologized and abandoned to special education programs and "alternative" schools after being marked with disability labels (Corporation for Educational Radio and Television, 1993).

In contrast to this, school marketization efforts in Milwaukee seemed to offer much more dignified subject positions to disenfranchised parents and guardians, perhaps most significantly that of *rational consumer*. Rather than pathologizing "Black" cultural forms through racist social scientific normative discourses, market-oriented voucher advocates first positioned parents and guardians as ideal consumers whose sole constraint consisted of artificially limited, market-defined choice. While positioning low-income parents and guardians of color as rational educational consumers empowered to make the best choices for their children dehistoricizes their agency by largely failing to see it as emerging within unequal material and discursive relations of power, neoliberal discourse at the same time allows parents and guardians to be seen, heard, and understood, and, perhaps most importantly, to act in ways that are often simply not possible within the everyday life of urban public schools.

An analysis predicated on questions of identify formation allows for the possibility of a micro-level examination of the tactical choices groups of parents and guardians make in negotiating their sets of perceived educational options on a terrain that is not largely of their own choosing. Rather than focusing only on the structural dynamics around educational marketization, which will likely further marginalize low-income urban communities of color (Lauder and Hughes, 1999; Whitty et al., 1998), I wish to follow Apple and Oliver's lead in taking seriously the everyday dilemmas, consciousness, and agency of voucher families as they attempt to negotiate educational structures that, intentionally or functionally, have not been designed with their best interests in mind (Apple, 1996; Apple & Oliver, 2003). Thus, although I am deeply concerned about the likely outcomes of market-oriented educational reforms in Milwaukee and elsewhere, I also want to take utterly seriously a consideration of how conservative educational mobilizations succeed by seeming to speak to marginalized people's very real fears and desires. It is through understanding this articulation, as a matter of identity formation and subaltern agency, that the process of conservative formation will perhaps most effectively be interrupted and supplanted with a more socially democratic (and ultimately more effective) educational vision.

Thus, seen from "below," from the vantage point of poor and working-class families of color, free market educational discourses seem to open a space to African American parents and guardians in interesting and contradictory ways (and in a manner not always present in the often pathologizing discourses of urban public schools). To approach this question of how offered subject positions are tactically "taken up" and "inhabited" by parents and guardians, we are aided by the work of critical cultural theorist Michel de Certeau. Although de Certeau problematically posits a monolithic sense of "power structure" (after all, in the case under examination, it is impossible to comfortably attribute the status of power structure to either the Milwaukee Public Schools and its allies or the pro-voucher forces), nevertheless a further engagement with his ideas will prove useful in examining the forms of agency with which African American parents and guardians negotiate their best interests.

In characterizing the mechanisms of power operating within the modern social formation, de Certeau (1984) endorses French theorist Michel Foucault's "microphysics of power," in which one finds "'miniscule' technical procedures acting on and with details, redistributing a discursive space in order to make it the means of a generalized 'discipline' (*surveillance)*" (p. xiv). Nevertheless, de Certeau faults Foucault's analysis for once again "privileg[ing] the productive apparatus" in failing to discover "how an entire society resists being reduced to [discipline]," and particularly "what popular procedures (also "miniscule" and quotidian) manipulate the mechanisms of discipline and conform to them in order to evade them" (p. xiv).

De Certeau uses the term *strategy* to identify a deployment of power to promote or maintain the interests of a power structure, and *tactics* to refer to the operations by which the less powerful defend or promote their interests. De Certeau's project is to make Foucault's analysis of power more complete, specifically by discerning an "anti-discipline" in the "ways of operating" that "constitute the innumerable practices by means of which users reappropriate the space organized by techniques of sociocultural production" (1984, p. xiv).

In the Milwaukee example, some disenfranchised African American "users" (that is, parents) negotiated the space of two powerful competing alliances, Milwaukee Public Schools and pro-voucher conservatives, deciding for tactical reasons, that at least for some, and at least in the short term, a conditional alliance with conservative forces represented greater opportunity than previously largely failed alliances with sympathetic forces within Milwaukee Public Schools. De Certeau would argue that parents and guardians are never passive or without agency within this process of alliance-building and subject formation. They, to use another one of his terms, "make do" within the identity options that are made available to them, turning subject positions as much as possible to purposes that they feel will best serve their educational and social interests (Apple, 1996; De Certeau, 1984).

Such a focus on identity formation as a component of subaltern agency allows us to discern that the articulations and alliances formed around vouchers in Milwaukee are much more transient, ephemeral, opportunistic, and unstable than current literature, including Apple and Oliver's "Becoming Right" piece (Apple, 1996; Apple & Oliver, 2003), implies (Apple & Pedroni, 2005). Nevertheless, despite the often transient nature of such conditional alliances, crucial and lasting gains are in fact won by educational conservatives as a result of the reforms that these alliances are able to engender. The effect of voucher mobilizations on legislation and on the global currency of private vouchers is not nearly as ephemeral as the conditional alliances that undergird and enable their initial success.

Therefore, as I argued earlier, a more nuanced theorization of groups such as the grassroots supporters of vouchers in Milwaukee—which cannot be adequately posited either as dominant elements within a hegemonic alliance or as relatively ideologically unformed and ordinary individuals articulated into the Right as a result of the state's intransigence—is crucial to the project of a fuller understanding of the Right's continued success in dismantling key vestiges of the American social democratic accord.

The current under-emphasis on the importance of subaltern agency in hegemonic successes might result from our inclination to theorize elements within conservative modernization as "groups" unproblematically embodying "ideal types," rather than as "discursive tendencies." Although some individuals and organizations can be more or less correctly categorized into one of Apple's four elements, there are also (almost) always contradictory tendencies within these groups and individuals. The fact that these tendencies are not embodied as ideal types (e.g., few groups or individuals are monolithically neoliberal or neoconservative), but rather are mediated in contradictory ways, actually expands conceptually the spaces for progressive rearticulation within the formation of these subjectivities.

Because we still want to foreground the ways in which these discourses construct and are constructed by real social actors, thus sidestepping the disposition of some post-structural theorists to see the world as made up only of competing discourses that somehow exist beyond history and human agency (Pedroni, 2005), we may want to refer to Apple's four elements as *embodied tendencies*. To not do so restricts our likelihood of apprehending the importance of subaltern groups in hegemonic successes because subaltern groups, unlike those closely aligned with more powerful embodied tendencies, often act tactically, in a manner suggested by de Certeau, and often not through the deployment of largely internally cohesive discourses that seek to (re)narrate a set of relationships between elements such as the state, the economy, individuals, and the social formation (De Certeau, 1984). The ability to materialize elaborate and cohesive intellectual discursive production is more typically a privilege of the powerful, who, as de Certeau suggests, shape and control the terrain upon which ideological and material battles over such things as access to education are fought. On the other hand, subaltern yet politically savvy groups, such as the African American and Latino supporters of private school vouchers in Milwaukee, quite often operate in a tactical relationship to power, sensing the need to act within the spaces that the powerful provide, sometimes in ways that creatively turn the strategic deployments of the powerful back against the powerful, and other times in ways that are ultimately self-defeating for subaltern groups, as powerful groups accomplish their objectives precisely *because of* tactical "poaching" by subaltern groups. This latter scenario, I would argue, is the far more likely long-term outcome of African American support of private school vouchers in Milwaukee.

In fact, my analysis in the next chapter of a series of interviews and observations of parents and guardians in a pilot project for this study indicates that this is indeed the case—African American articulation to neoliberal interventions including voucher programs seems to be largely tactical and opportunistic, rather than strategic and ideologically disciplined.

3

THE MOVEMENT TO THE MARKET:

MAKING DO ON A POST-BROWN TERRAIN

If the parents say, "You know what? Choice is a good thing!" And they begin to vote out of office all of those politicians who got in office largely because the unions open up their phone banks and their bank account, then what you might see—listen to me carefully—you might see a radical realignment of American politics. Most people look at it as Left-Right, Democrat-Republican. The fact of the matter is, in America, Black folks have ... the only way to get things done is through the good auspices of powerful White folks, beginning with the Abolitionists. Black folks in America have only been the difference on contested ground. And the Democrats largely—liberals largely—have been the biggest supporters of Blacks. And in return for that, they—liberals, Democrats—want Blacks' undying loyalty. Well, it happens to be that a major part of the liberal Democrats are the unions. Now the unions were with us in the Civil Rights struggle. They have been our allies. They are simply not our allies today because we threaten their way of life. [Applause from audience.] The root fear is not that we will succeed in the school choice movement. It is that we will successfully effect a political realignment which will take all of their sacred cows down.

**Author's transcription, BAEO 2001 plenary session,
"The Revolution Will Not Be Televised"**

As I argued in the last chapter, and as will be evident in the following brief analysis of interviews conducted by a conservative videographer supported by the Bradley Foundation, African American voucher advocates rarely offer "intact" neoliberal or neoconservative discourses as underpinning their investment in vouchers. Although their discourses include occasional neoliberal and neoconservative elements, they also contain other elements that run significantly counter to each of these discourses. Because of their tactical relationship to dominant groups, and because of their investment in other mobilizations that are in clear opposition to the project of conservative modernization, African American supporters of vouchers in Milwaukee (and I believe this will manifest itself more broadly) do not typically "become Right" in terms of identity formation, despite their tactical investment in neoconservative and neoliberal subject positions (Apple, 1996; Apple & Oliver, 2003). Two brief examples from the pilot project in Milwaukee will help illustrate this point.

Listening to African American Voucher Families in Milwaukee

Cherise Robinson and Laura Fordham (their names have been changed to preserve their anonymity) are African American parents and guardians of children utilizing vouchers provided through the MPCP to attend participating parochial and nonsectarian private schools. The interviews from which I draw this brief analysis were recorded in 1998 shortly before the Wisconsin Supreme Court upheld the constitutionality of the MPCP, thus lifting an appeals court injunction predicated on issues of separation of church and state.[1] The two interviews, conducted by a Bradley Foundation-supported European-American professional videographer closely affiliated with neoconservative Catholic educational organizations in Milwaukee, took place in Madison, Wisconsin, shortly after a well-publicized speak-out and rally among voucher proponents protesting the injunction (phone interview with videographer, April 22, 2000).

Cherise Robinson is the grandmother of a 5-year-old child who began the school year in a private nonsectarian school participating in the Milwaukee voucher program. Her granddaughter was soon relocated to a public day care facility after the voucher school in which she was enrolled "had to close before the year was up." Despite this disruption, Ms. Robinson is stridently positive about her granddaughter's advances in her initial months of private school attendance. "If you were to talk to her, you would think that she's about 7 or 8 years old. And judging from the other children that are in Milwaukee Public Schools, she's at a level now of at least a second or third grader. And I know that this is because of her beginnings."

Robinson attributes this success to the existence of small class sizes and greater individual attention—which she identifies as lacking in many of Milwaukee's urban public schools. "I think it's because of the individual attention that she's able to get in the private schools. And not so much individual, but not so many students. That the teacher has more time for her in whatever her little situation may be."

Implicit in Robinson's assessment is a juxtaposition of the attentive private school teacher with the less attending public school teacher. That which facilitates the better attention of the private school teacher, however, is that she has "not so many students"; she does not face the same overcrowded classroom conditions as her public school counterpart. This implicit characterization of the public school teacher beset by overcrowding contrasts markedly with the figure of the public teacher in the interviewer's own narrative, in which public schools are seen as failing not because of overcrowded classrooms, but because of their monopolization by teachers' unions, which protect unworthy teachers while sheltering grossly bloated and inefficient school bureaucracies from market discipline.

An indictment of overcrowded classrooms, rather than union monopolies and a lack of competitive educational markets, points to a diagnosis and prescription for public schools that can only sit awkwardly within the neoliberal frame of "market efficiency/inefficiency." The awkwardness of this articulation is tempered only by considerable work, which allows for a type of hegemonic suturing (Apple, 1996) that never resolves the inhering contradictions.

However, this is not the only juncture at which Ms. Robinson's frame exists in tense relationship with that of the interviewer and the various fragments of the neoliberal and neoconservative voucher alliance with which he is allied. Robinson describes her active defense of the voucher program as follows: "It seems as if there are some who say that certain children shouldn't have a certain type of education. And it seems to me that choice is saying every child should have the best education that they can get." Robinson understands choice as the ability of every child, regardless of socioeconomic or other circumstances, to obtain high quality education. This sense of choice is articulated with models of consumer choice in marketization discourses only as the result of considerable work.

The daughter of the second interview subject, Laura Fordham, attends a private nonsectarian elementary school in which her mother also works as the admissions chairperson. For Ms. Fordham, the overriding factor in using a voucher to choose this particular school is its proximity to the family's home. In Milwaukee, this is not an inconsequential issue. With the advent of busing, many public neighborhood schools in the urban core were closed. This has presented significant difficulties related not just to the daily transportation of children; distance has also formed a significant obstacle to parental involvement in the public schools, particularly when many families do not own cars. This in turn has exacerbated the sense that public schools are frequently out of touch with the communities they serve.

As Ms. Fordham explains, "If she has to go back to the public schools, then she would be bused possibly across town. Well, I would not allow for her to be bused across town. First thing's, she's a chronic asthmatic kid. And for her to be bused, it would be impossible." Ms. Fordham's decision to relocate her child to a neighborhood private school came only after considerable effort to make the public school option work. "I could not transport her to school back and forward every day. I did that for her first year ... that was seventeen and a half miles away. So when she become more chronically ill, and my husband becomes ill, she had to stop going to school there, because I couldn't take her to school. Plus we couldn't afford it."

Ms. Fordham is nostalgic for a time "when the schools were so much better than they are now, the public schools at least. ... You could go to school down the street and meet your neighbors." That is, public schools were also important centers of life within the community. "Now, the way the [public] schools are going, they tell you where your kid can go. Where with the Choice program, you're able to put your kid ... where you want them to go. ... And you're able to afford it." Today in Milwaukee, private voucher-accepting neighborhood schools are often called upon by parents and guardians to fulfill the community role the neighborhood public schools once played. "And that's important, because we find that for our private schools are closer around in the circle than public schools are."

Beyond the absence of public schools within some Milwaukee urban neighborhoods, Ms. Fordham also characterizes the experiences of many public school children in the following way: "They are in the classroom, and they're crowded. And if a kid is a little slower learning he [doesn't] have the time to take ... so after a while he'll just stop going to school, or he'll miss school because he didn't know his lesson, or he had nobody to pay attention to him." Ms. Fordham's description of public school classrooms as overcrowded and under-resourced resonates with earlier criticisms by

Ms. Robinson. Her assumptions concerning the troubles of some urban public schools differ sharply from those of the interviewer and the neoliberal and neoconservative constituencies he represents.

This divergence of assumptions between Ms. Fordham and the interviewer is further evident as they negotiate the content of the interview. For example, in relation to the issue of consumer choice within educational markets, he asks, "Why should that be your choice? As a parent, or as a grandparent, or as a family member, why should you have the right to [choose] that?" Although the interviewer positions Ms. Fordham as a consumer within an educational marketplace, she answers from a very different subject position—that of a member within a community and society: "One of the things I feel is going to improve our society is if we can educate our kids better." Again, Ms. Fordham's "parent as community member" sits awkwardly with the interviewer's own "parent as consumer."

Disarticulation and Rearticulation

These brief excerpts represent, at the micro-level, an important instantiation of the tense, contradictory, and often successful process of articulation and conditional alliance-building within the movement for vouchers. Although the tensions and contradictions in such articulations are vividly evidenced in the differing purposes, resources, and identities that the interviewer and the two interview participants bring to the interviews, clearly they also share a limited common purpose that allows them to stand together "in the same room," however awkwardly. Both the interviewer (as a neoliberal and neoconservative advocate of educational marketization and Catholic schools) and the interview subjects (as parents and guardians concerned about their children's education) are interested in furthering at least a specific, limited version of "parental choice" in Milwaukee. One can imagine that these parents and guardians, in contrast to the interviewer, are unlikely to favor "choice" beyond the low-income parameters within which it was initially established.

In significant ways, then, the subaltern and tactical agency that Ms. Robinson, Ms. Fordham, and other African American parents, guardians, and community leaders I interviewed have demonstrated within the contested terrain over vouchers (see Chapter 5), is a testament to the strength of their potential political agency, rather than, as is sometimes suggested, an indication of naïve submission to hegemonic conservative educational and economic discourses. This remains true even if these parents, guardians, and community leaders are ultimately proven wrong in their assertions that their actions will be of maximum benefit in the long run not just for their children but also for other children left behind in newly market-disciplined urban public schools. This tactical agency will, in all likelihood, be further instantiated in future mobilizations, quite possibly around other traditionally conservative themes, many of which have long been issues of concern for large numbers of African American families, including support for school prayer and "religious freedom," as well as antipathy toward abortion and the interests of sexual minorities. African Americans (as well as other subaltern groups) are not essential Democrats, although in recent history many have tactically aligned themselves with this party. Critical theorists and others on the educational left should recognize that African American articulation to the Democratic Party and other powerful, liberal, progressive, and centrist groups has almost always been tactical. To theorize African Americans as "intelligent" when they show unquestioning loyalty to the Democratic Party and other liberal causes, even when these take their support for granted as they drift to the Right on significant issues, and "foolish" when they tactically participate in other, sometimes more conservative, alliances (such as that around vouchers) grossly misrepresents African American agency, and betrays what I feel is a racist essentialization of Black intelligence. Subaltern groups have always needed to tactically associate in seemingly contradictory ways with powerful groups and individuals, such as the Heritage Foundation, the Bradley Foundation, and the Democratic Leadership Council, in order to seek to protect their interests.

This point is reinforced by an examination of the rich debate among generations of African Americans over *the relative advantages* of nationalist and integrationist reform strategies at particular historical conjunctures (e.g., Dyson, 1993, pp. 115–128; Fanon, 1967, pp. 83–108; Jones, 1985; Marable & Mullings, 2000; West, 1982, pp. 131–147). In his excellent history of Black school reform movements in Milwaukee, Dougherty challenges what he terms the "abandonment narrative" regarding tensions between integrationists and separatists, arguing instead that Milwaukee's own school integration movement

> did not arise as a united front but rather as a diverse coalition of participants with different motivations. While all became members of the same movement, there was not a universal ideology cohering their

disparate views, experiences, and expectations. Some activists joined because of their strong commitment to building an integrated society, but others took part because they saw the integration strategy as the best path toward gaining better resources for black schooling, strengthening black cultural identity, or challenging white supremacy. (Dougherty 2004, p. 107)

As the quote that opened this chapter suggests, these debates over tactics are just as real and present today as they were during the building of coalitions in support of the *Brown* case 50 years ago. And it is precisely in times of *unsettlement*, that is, in moments of profound flux in discourses and processes related to the state (witness the current flux in the nature of the welfare state, discussed earlier), that real polyvocality emerges within marginalized communities over the direction of subaltern energies. This polyvocality is also evident in treatises concerning the state of Black education today, as varying trajectories regarding multiculturalism and Afrocentrism, separatism and hybridity, coexist in discursive proximity (e.g., Ginwright, 2004; King, 2005; Major, 2001; Rofes & Stulberg, 2004).

Reflecting on the pivotal role played by subaltern groups, I want to suggest that the conservative hegemonic alliance in the late 1980s recognized that it *almost* wielded the power to get vouchers through. Although by itself the hegemonic alliance was not able (yet) to successfully realize its marketization agenda concerning education and vouchers, the Right could "stretch" its power by bringing parts of a traditional liberal constituency—a portion of African American low-income families—on board. Articulating the privatization agenda in education to these parents' and guardians' "good sense" and perceived interests, including a long-standing desire for "community control" of schools, would enable the Right to tip the scales of educational power away from an alliance of liberal groups, including teachers' unions, other trade unions, the American Civil Liberties Union, People for the American Way, the National Association for the Advancement of Colored People, the Urban League, and feminist and environmental organizations, and toward the amalgamation of groups pursuing conservative modernization in education. Given the Wisconsin political climate of the late 1980s, in which progressives wielded very little power, coupled with a long and historic movement among African American families in Milwaukee for community-controlled schools that would protect their children from the sometimes reprehensible racial practices of

Milwaukee Public Schools, Milwaukee presented itself as an ideal battle-ground upon which the conservative alliance might win crucial ideological battles over the character, form, and funding of education in the United States (Carl, 1996). Such a victory would also have promising implications for farther-reaching conservative goals involving the broad privatization of the public sphere and the "deresponsibilization" of the state.

In the process, the immediate and long-term conservative agendas around privatization in education and elsewhere would not be the only part of the hegemonic project that would be served. It will be useful here to reinvoke the conceptualization Michael Apple has proposed of the conservative hegemonic alliance as constituted through a series of tensely negotiated and maintained compromises among disparate but overlapping powerful interests (Apple, 1993, 1996, 2001), or what I have proposed calling discursive tendencies. In regard to the contestation of such a tense alliance, critical theorists in education and elsewhere have correctly argued that one strategy to forward the agenda of a radically democratic social and educational project might be to carefully discern these fault lines within the hegemonic alliance so that potential tensions among the different positions might be exacerbated, thereby pushing the project of conservative modernization in the direction of crisis. Just as progressives hope to strategically promote their interests through capitalizing on these points of suture on the Right, so too the Right has an interest in continuing to capitalize on and subvert tensions among real and potential progressive allies.

One of the fault lines that the Right seems to have successfully discerned and targeted is the articulation within what we might call the traditional progressive alliance between African American groups and teachers' unions such as the National Education Association (NEA) and the American Federation of Teachers (AFT). By infusing the common sense of the United States social formation with narrativized images of self-interested teachers' unions protecting their own jobs and "enriching" themselves, with little concern for the students of color who increasingly make up our public school populations, the Right may be succeeding in destroying residual elements of a progressive alliance at the same time that it strengthens its own ascendancy (Holt, 2000). Calls by national teachers' unions for the improvement of teachers' working conditions through "zero tolerance" in student discipline have likely only contributed to these tensions. Regarding this disarticulation between teachers' unions and African

American parents and guardians, I want to assert that a careful appraisal of such educational dynamics in contexts such as Milwaukee will be quite instructive in both the theorization and the contestation of this process of disarticulation among potential and actual progressive allies.

For many African American urban leaders who have, sometimes even tepidly, supported vouchers, the reaction of some progressive Whites has been quite illuminating. It is characteristically a reaction whereby, previously content to see Blacks as "wisely" coalescing with predominantly White progressive initiatives, they now see these same Blacks as foolishly allying themselves with dangerous forces. A tacit message appears to be that Blacks don't know the real dangers of allying with "reprehensible" conservative people; only White liberals know that. It smacks of a feeling of the "White man's burden," where liberal White educators are now angry at the "Black children" who they had gathered under their umbrella, because those children are showing independence of mind.

Conclusions

In this and the preceding chapter I have utilized a conceptual and empirical discussion of the discursive overlaps, tensions, and power differentials among constituents of the Milwaukee voucher alliance to suggest the importance of subaltern agency and identity formation within the process of conservative formation. Based on the conceptual and empirical juxtapositions in which I engaged, I argued for an expansion and reconceptualization of the theories of conservative modernization offered by Apple and Oliver in their essay, "Becoming Right." The modifications I have proposed incorporate processes of identity formation and subaltern agency among "strange bedfellows" as key components of the fragile and uneven process through which conservative educational mobilizations experience varying degrees of success or failure.

I have argued that the success and maintenance of such educational projects is predicated neither on a direct imposition of a conservative educational agenda onto unwitting and passive subaltern populations (e.g., voucher parents and guardians), nor on the "welling up from below" of a reified [parental] identity that somehow fits seamlessly into conservative educational mobilizations. Rather, utilizing but also expanding Michael Apple's theories of conservative modernization, I have pointed to the formation of fleeting and conditional alliances among differently empowered and socially situated social actors. Within this process there is always a highly structurally and discursively limited agency on the part of those dispossessed mobilized over the issue of their consent, as well as a contested discursive space within which potentially more socially democratic articulations and educational visions might be formed.

It is my hope that this retheorization builds upon Apple's crucial work in helping critical educators envision strategies for rearticulating marginalized families' educational concerns to ultimately more effective, meaningful, and democratic educational reform. Hopefully, the conceptual modifications that evidence such as the interviews with voucher parents and guardians suggest, will assist researchers in other contexts to discern similar processes and trajectories. We can imagine that tactical investments in fleeting conservative alliances and subject positions among marginalized communities will play an increasingly significant role both in the United States and elsewhere.

In the following chapters I begin to analyze the ethnographic data collected in terms of the processes of articulation and identity formation that are in motion at both a macro- and micro-level.

4

THE PROMISED LAND AND
THE SUPERMARKET:
LEADERSHIP ON AN
UNSETTLING TERRAIN

I arrive at the downtown Milwaukee Hilton, a tall, elegant brick structure built in the 1930s, to attend the day's events associated with the first
annual national symposium of the Black Alliance for Educational Options
(BAEO). Leaving the parking ramp, I enter the hotel's opulent lobby, and
ascend an elegant spiral staircase toward the sound of a booming African
American speaker's voice. I recognize the voice as that of Howard Fuller,
the keynote speaker of the opening event, and the founder of BAEO and
the Institute for the Transformation of Learning (ITL) at Marquette
University. Fuller, whose advocacy for radical reform in Black education
dates back to the militancy of the Black Power movement in the 1960s,
has since the late 1980s been a leading voice nationally and internationally
in the call for vouchers for low-income parents. His previous experiences
have included a term as superintendent of Milwaukee Public Schools in
the early 1990s, and he is now infamous within left-liberal educational
circles for helping to forge a pioneering—some would say heretical—alliance between African American organizations and Right-wing foundations and think-tanks, including Bradley, Heritage, and Friedman.

With these reflections in mind I arrive at the top of the spiral stair-case and enter the Hilton's Crystal Ballroom, a very large and elegant room with ornate crystal chandeliers and approximately 50 large circu-lar tables. Fuller has just begun addressing the assembled participants, about 500 in number, who are overwhelmingly African American and extremely well dressed in suits and ties, formal dresses, and long color-ful African robes.

Taking a seat in the first chair I find, I am struck by Fuller's elo-quence, as well as the passion of his oratory style. He delivers his tes-timony in the cadences of a Black Baptist preacher, his head and body swaying from side to side as he speaks, evoking exclamations of "alright" and "yes, tell it" from many of the seated participants.

Fuller quotes large tracts of the revolutionary Brazilian educator Paolo Freire from memory, citing passage after passage from the *Peda-gogy of the Oppressed*. He weaves Freire's words together with a blistering condemnation of relations of power along racial lines in education in the United States, stating that through America's schools, "One group is being prepared to run the world, while the other is being prepared to take orders from those who run the world." Fuller castigates afflu-ent Whites for their retreat into gated communities and laments the waste, narrow profitability, and ethical bankruptcy of America's prison-industrial society. He criticizes public school teachers who, accord-ing to Fuller, feel that, "My check's gonna come whether you learn or not." This criticism is also extended to White liberal reformers, who are always ready to construct a "new 5-year plan that will at some point get to you," while the lives of Black schoolchildren are flowing down the drain right now.

For Fuller, the issue is not "choice," but who has it. Most White and affluent Americans already have school choice; most poor and Black parents, because of their financial limitations, do not. These parents, according to Fuller, only want the choice that other Americans already possess. Vouchers enable this.

Fuller summons his audience to maintain courage in their move-ment because, "We're going to be called names and lose friends." Fur-thermore, this is "not a struggle for the faint of heart," in particular because "wresting power from established [educational and civil rights] organizations will never come easy." But, "anything worth having takes a sacrifice; nothing precious comes easy."

Fuller then responds to critics who have argued that Black voucher advocates are "duped by the Right wing." Fuller reminds his audience that BAEO is controlled by Black people, and not by anyone else, but that, "we are grateful to White people with money who have supported us." Fuller refers to BAEO's alliance with Right-wing organizations as "a partnership." "We have an agenda, they support it, and so we welcome them." But, "we will never be dictated to by them."

He criticizes Blacks who are nervous about BAEO's association with Right-wing groups, calling them people who "still fear White people." They argue to Fuller that, "you're going to be co-opted." To them, Fuller answers: "Why do you think that? Why is it that you don't think we have the capacity to go in [to meetings with these organizations] and come out with our agenda being supported?"

Fuller receives thunderous applause as he comments that, "if a Black person supports something Right-wing, they're dupes. If they support something liberal, they're called brilliant. Then I'm brilliantly duped."

He sharply criticizes liberal Whites who argue that the voucher program will leave the neediest behind in urban public schools, and asks, "Why do you ask that question, when you left us behind [in urban public schools]?" He points to the hypocrisy of critics who argue that a move away from public schools to private schools will destroy integration, and that public schools represent the chance for all races and classes to get together. "I don't think so!" Fuller intones forcefully, "The only people getting together there is us!"

Fuller closes by citing the radical Black abolitionist Frederick Douglass: "If there is no struggle, there is no progress." People who want progress without struggle "want the rain without the thunder and lightning." Finally, "power concedes nothing without a demand."

Author's field notes, March 2, 2001

The Emergence of the Black Alliance for Educational Options (BAEO)

One of the most significant organizations to emerge around the issue of voucher advocacy among urban poor and working class communities of color has been the BAEO. According to its former executive director, Kaleem Caire, BAEO was formed in August 2000, in order to represent a distinctly Black voice in the voucher debates, and in particular within the alliance pushing voucher-based educational reform, both in

Milwaukee and nationally. Although BAEO supports "parental choice" in education in various forms—it favors the development of charter schools, magnet schools, public school choice, and home schooling, among other options—the primary purpose of the organization, according to Caire, is to advocate for publicly financed private school vouchers for low-income parents in urban settings (phone interview, February 25, 2001).

BAEO has attracted significant attention not just for its iconoclasm in aligning itself with traditionally conservative organizations in support- ing conservative educational reform, but also for accepting funding from a variety of conservative foundations and think-tanks that are not usu- ally thought of as having the best interests of urban Blacks in mind. Past and current contributors that BAEO has listed on its website include the Bradley Foundation, the Friedman Foundation, and the Walton Family Foundation. Among BAEO contributors, the Bradley Foundation is per- haps the most notorious for funding the 1994 best-selling volume *The Bell Curve*, which gathered allegedly scientific evidence to establish the inher- ent mental inferiority of African Americans to both Whites and Asians (People for the American Way [PFAW], 2001). More will be said about BAEO's funding later.

I began this chapter with a journal passage excerpting Howard Fuller's speech at the 2001 Symposium of the BAEO as a fitting way of opening a chapter in which I hope to demonstrate the complexity of the discur- sive and social political node that BAEO as an organization occupies. The awareness that Fuller shows of his critics, his allies, and the limited range of educational options within which low-income African American families must act seems to already belie the notion, put forward by some (e.g., PFAW, 2001), that BAEO is simply a front organization for the educational Right.

Although in portions of his talk Fuller foregrounds the neoliberal subject position of an individuated Black parent who makes choices as a consumer within an educational marketplace, and explains that "freedom expresses itself in decision," there are also sections of his speech, such as his references to Freire's *Pedagogy of the Oppressed*, that reflect an intimacy with critical Left literature in education and other fields (Freire, 1993).

This fusion between Left and neoliberal critique of current relations of educational and social power in the United States, coupled with themes clearly derived from the historical struggles of African Americans to end race-based oppression, serves as evidence that Fuller's (and BAEO's) positions on educational reform cannot simply be dismissed as conservative talking points delivered in "Blackface."

In this chapter, I divide my analysis of the BAEO into two distinct steps. First, I examine the articulations that have been formed within BAEO itself as an alliance of differently interested and differently empowered social and educational actors. Next, I look at the articulations that have been formed between BAEO and various other members of the voucher alliance.

Articulations within BAEO at the Level of Leadership

As the second term in its name implies, the BAEO is not an organization disciplined by a singular set of ideologies regarding the intersection of education, race, and inequality. Despite the public image that the organization typically presents, there are in fact significant differences that structure organizational life within BAEO. In some ways, the qualities that differentiate various constituencies within the organization parallel the complexity of what White liberals and others often misleadingly refer to as "the Black community." That is, BAEO is comprised of individuals and organizations that vary in wealth, education, political belief, religiosity, and access to financial, political, and symbolic resources. Furthermore, although some members clearly have a direct financial interest in particular "educational options," others seem to be motivated mainly by social justice commitments.

Although founded in Milwaukee, Wisconsin, BAEO's board of directors at the time of this writing is comprised of 27 members in 21 cities (BAEO website). A recent study by PFAW, (2001) reports that BAEO's board of directors includes "many high-profile advocates, such as former representative Floyd Flake (D-NY) and right-wing radio host Armstrong Williams. Some, like J. Kenneth Blackwell and Dwight Evans, are elected state officials. Others have made a career in working in charter or voucher schools or in private management companies that stand to gain from privatization of public schools" (PFAW, 2001).

Dr. Howard Fuller is BAEO's founder and chair. BAEO grew out of meetings of African American parents, community leaders, and educational reformers that Fuller organized through Marquette University's Institute for the Transformation of Learning in the late 1980s, where he has also been professor since 1995. Not only had Fuller served as superintendent of Milwaukee Public Schools earlier in that decade, he had also worked as the primary organizer for an independent Black school district on Milwaukee's north side in the late 1980s (BAEO website; PFAW, 2001). Fuller also has deep roots in the Civil Rights movement, the Black Power movement, and in Pan-Africanism (interview with author, June 30, 2003).

Kaleem Caire, who served as executive director of BAEO during the time of this research, had previously acted as director of the Wisconsin Center for Academically Talented Youth, and as an educational consultant for the Wisconsin Department of Public Instruction. In 2000 he received a Martin Luther King, Jr. Humanitarian Award from the city of Madison, Wisconsin, for his work around issues of educational quality. Recently Caire has worked for the American Education Reform Council and Fight for Children, a Washington, D.C.-based organization that advocates for programs supporting "at risk" and low-income students in the nation's capital (personal communication, April 2003).

Although many, perhaps even most, of BAEO's board members have fairly organic educational connections to low-income communities of color in major urban centers across the United States, a few board members have explicit connections to (other) Right-wing causes or to companies that would potentially benefit from implementation of some of the options for which BAEO advocates. For example, Deborah McGriff, Howard Fuller's wife, is, at the time of this writing, president of Edison Teacher's College, a subsidiary of the for-profit educational entity, Edison Schools, Inc. As of November 1999, she was reported to hold $3 million in Edison stock options (PFAW, 2001). Former New York Democratic representative and BAEO board member Floyd Flake serves as president of Edison Charter Schools, another Edison Schools entity. Like McGriff, he could potentially benefit financially from the further privatization of public school systems (PFAW, 2001; BAEO website). Kenneth Campbell, also a BAEO board member, is vice president for Business Development for Mosaica Education, Inc., another for-profit private education corporation. In 2001, Mosaica Education acquired Advantage Schools, Inc., for which Campbell had been working at the time of the acquisition (BAEO website).

The BAEO board also includes right-wing radio personality Armstrong Williams, host of the nationally syndicated *The Right Side* and *The Armstrong Williams Show*. Williams is a vocal critic of affirmative action policies and gay rights. He has worked for conservative Supreme Court Justice Clarence Thomas and for formerly segregationist Republican

Senator Strom Thurmond (BAEO website; PFAW, 2001). BAEO board member Kenneth Blackwell served as undersecretary of the Department of Housing and Urban Development during the first Bush administration, and is a prominent Republican and contributor to Alan Keyes' right-wing Black America's Political Action Committee, or BAMPAC (PFAW, 2001; BAEO website). Taunya Young served as an administrator for Golden Christian Academy, which was expelled from the Cleveland voucher program after it was discovered that the school conducted all classroom instruction through videos targeted toward Christian homeschoolers (PFAW, 2001; BAEO website). Jacqueline Joyner-Cissell is the president of the Indianapolis Chapter of Right to Life, and the first president of Black Family Forum, which, according to BAEO's website, promotes "a more conservative view regarding black families." She also sits on the board of directors of BAMPAC (BAMPAC website).

The presence of socially conservative advocacy groups and market-interested educational companies and their representatives is also apparent in the list of speakers and workshop facilitators at BAEO's annual symposia. For example, not only are BAEO board members Deborah McGriff and Floyd Flake employees of Edison Schools, but in the first three annual symposia, the following Edison representatives also had the opportunity to impact BAEO through symposium presentations: Miata Fuller, vice president for Charter Development at Edison Schools, and Howard Fuller's daughter (2001); Jeannie Ullrich, vice president of Edison Teachers College (2001); Sandra Robinson, Edison Schools spokesperson (2001); Kimberly Motley Brand, Detroit Edison Public Schools (2001); Jan Gillespie, Edison Schools representative (2002); David Graff, Edison Schools spokesperson (2002); Dwayne Andrews, Edison Schools spokesperson (2003); Adrian Morgan, Edison Schools spokesperson (2003); Cynthia Robbins, Edison Schools spokesperson (2003); and finally, Ricardo Weir, principal of Edison Medrano Academy in Dallas, Texas (2003) (BAEO symposia programs and author's field notes, 2001, 2002, 2003).

Edison is not the only private for-profit educational corporation that has a significant presence at BAEO symposia. Not only is Kenneth Campbell of Mosaica Education, Inc. on BAEO's board, but Sheila Royal Moses, a colleague of Campbell during his time at Advantage Schools, also presented at the 2001 symposium in Milwaukee, as did Thomas Stewart of LearnNow, Inc. (since merged into Edison Schools) (BAEO symposia programs and author's field notes, 2001, 2002, 2003).

Other more socially conservative groups and individuals, although not on BAEO's board, have had a significant presence at the symposia. Sherry Street of the American Education Reform Council, U.S. Secretary of Education Rod Paige, Clint Bolick of the Institute for Justice, and Brian Carpenter of the Mackinac Center for Public Policy have all been featured presenters at recent BAEO symposia (BAEO symposia programs and author's field notes, 2001, 2002, 2003). More will be said about BAEO's relationship with these organizations and individuals later.

It would be facile and reductive to conclude that these market-oriented and socially conservative individuals and groups dominate BAEO. BAEO's board also contains individuals with significant progressive credentials (PFAW, 2001; BAEO website; author interview with Howard Fuller, June 30, 2003), including the following:

- Dale Sadler, a well-known Colorado-based civil rights attorney.
- William Breazell, who has served as president of the Colorado Springs NAACP.
- Amber Blackwell, who headed the drive in Oakland, California to create New Village charter school, whose mission was to teach about tolerance by exploring issues of race, class, and sexual orientation in the curriculum.
- Pennsylvania State Representative Dwight Evans, a lifelong Democrat with an enduring affiliation and friendship with the state's teachers unions.
- T. Willard Fair, president and chief executive officer of the Urban League of Greater Miami, Inc. Fair has worked for the Urban League since 1963, and has served as an adjunct professor of Social Work at the National Urban League's Whitney M. Young, Jr., Center for Urban Leadership.
- Mashea Ashton, the Midwest regional director of KIPP schools, a progressive non-profit network of charter schools serving marginalized urban communities. Ashton's scholarly work in the sociology of education has focused on uncovering and interrogating the disproportionate number of children of color who are designated for special education classes. She has also engaged in research on promoting educational access and full inclusion for students with disabilities.

Despite the presence of these progressive board members, it is undeniable that market-oriented and socially conservatives groups and individuals have a significant presence within BAEO. The implication of this, however, is not that BAEO is a puppet organization for the Right, educationally or otherwise. Rather, BAEO is an alliance of differently interested and differentially empowered African American educational actors, many of whom have significant relationships with broader neoliberal and neo-conservative forces in American society. Ultimately, though, what unites BAEO's leadership is not rightist political and educational ideology, but rather a mutual interest in specific limited programs of educational choice and vouchers.

Articulations between BAEO and Other Members of the Pro-Voucher Alliance

In the previous section I described some of the political, social, and commercial affiliations of board members and symposium presenters within BAEO. In a sense, these affiliations mark divergent interests, politics, beliefs, and access to resources of various kinds *within* BAEO. In this section, I turn to the relationships BAEO has forged with organizations and tendencies that are located more *outside* of BAEO. Of course, it is difficult to draw a strict boundary between tendencies within BAEO and tendencies outside of it, given that membership within BAEO is comprised of individuals and organizations that are also part of the "outside" organizations.

Nevertheless, I want to contend that the groups and individuals discussed in this section are ones with which BAEO negotiates its interests strategically as a singular organization, despite the internal differences within BAEO. They are its "partners" in the alliance, with whom there are both significant overlaps and tensions in regard to educational and social agendas.

It will be useful to make an analytical distinction at this point between the foundations that *fund* the BAEO and the organizations and tendencies that *ally* themselves with BAEO's educational agenda. I call this distinction analytical, as opposed to simply empirical, because it would be reasonable to assume that those who fund BAEO also share, at least to an extent, its educational agenda. Nevertheless separating sources of funding from sources of solidarity allows us to approach an analysis of BAEO from a position that takes BAEO's claims regarding its autonomy and its agency within the voucher alliance seriously. That is, BAEO's claim is that it chooses its *allies* based on shared purpose, and its *funders* based simply on their willingness and ability to contribute without strings attached (author's interview with Kaleem Caire, March 5, 2001).

I turn to those who finance BAEO first, reserving a discussion of BAEO's allies for later in the chapter. As mentioned earlier, BAEO grew out of a series of meetings organized by Dr. Howard Fuller at the Institute for the Transformation of Learning at Marquette University in Milwaukee. These initial meetings were funded, at least in part, by a $30,000 grant from the Friedman Foundation, founded in 1996 by free market fundamentalists Milton and Rose Friedman in order to promote marketized forms of educational provision to replace the supposed inefficiency of state educational monopolies. The Friedman Foundation also donated $230,000 in 2000 for BAEO's first campaign of television and radio commercials (PFAW, 2001).

BAEO began in August 2000, with a $900,000 operating budget provided by the Walton Family Foundation. Under Wal-Mart heir John Walton, the Walton Family Foundation has funded pro-voucher think-tanks such as the Goldwater Institute and the Manhattan Institute for Policy Research. Walton also contributed significantly to a number of failed state voucher initiatives, including $2 million to the 2000 Michigan initiative, $250,000 to California's 1993 Proposition 174, and unspecified amounts to the 1997 Minnesota voucher campaign. The Walton Family Foundation, along with the Bradley Foundation, has provided financial support for the defense of the Milwaukee and Cleveland voucher programs, litigated by the right-wing Landmark Legal Foundation and the Institute for Justice. Additionally, Walton has contributed over $14 million to institutions that grant private educational "scholarships" to low-income children, which are believed to help boost the credibility of vouchers as a "common" educational phenomenon (PFAW, 2001).

However, the most significant foundation for BAEO has been the Milwaukee-based Lynde and Harry Bradley Foundation, which has been the nation's foremost conservative donor over the last two decades. Between 1985 and 1999, under the leadership of Michael Joyce, Bradley has provided grants totaling more than $355 million, mostly to right-wing think-tanks and other conservative causes. Grants totaling $11 million and $14.5 million, respectively, have been awarded by Bradley to the Heritage Foundation and the American Enterprise Institute (Media Transparency, 2003). Bradley has also donated $4.5 million to David Horowitz's Center for the Study of Popular Culture, which has purchased ads in campus newspapers claiming that the idea of reparations for slavery was a racist one, and that Blacks in the United States should be grateful for the gift of "the highest standard of living of blacks anywhere in the world" (Media Transparency, 2003; PFAW, 2001).

Bradley also funds a number of other organizations that advocate for "parental choice" measures, including tuition tax credits, such as the Center for Education Reform ($380,000), the Heartland Institute ($118,000), the Claremont Institute ($2.5 million), the Free Congress Foundation ($6.4 million), and the American Education Reform Council ($1.2 million) (Media Transparency, 2003). To Milwaukee's voucher movement, Bradley had, as of June 2001, earmarked $1.7 million for Howard Fuller's Institute for the Transformation of Learning. Additionally, Bradley provided $350,000 to the State of Wisconsin for the defense of the state's voucher program by former independent counsel Kenneth Starr, after it came under legal challenge over issues of separation of church and state (Media Transparency, 2003; PFAW, 2001).

According to a perusal of the 1,251 Bradley grants listed on Media Transparency's website, the foundation has contributed meaningful amounts to most of the "flagship" Milwaukee Parental Choice Schools, including one in this study (Media Transparency, 2003). These contributions have ranged from tens of thousands of dollars to millions of dollars. (Such contributions, it should be noted, should cast doubt upon claims neoliberals might make regarding the salutary effects of "free market" forces in the event that the MPCP is able to produce positive "academic returns." Any such success would be at least partially attributable to subsidization by grant-makers. The notion that schools would need additional non-market derived capital, and not just placement within a competitive market, is one that belies the case typically made by neoliberal voucher advocates.)

As of 2003, Bradley has also contributed $14.5 million dollars to Partners Advancing Values in Education (PAVE), a Milwaukee-based organization that provided private vouchers to low-income children for private sectarian school attendance while that aspect of the MPCP was under an injunction of the Wisconsin Court of Appeals, between 1995 and 1998. Finally, Bradley has contributed at least $600,000 directly to BAEO (Media Transparency, 2003).

BAEO also lists among its contributors the following foundations and organizations: the VCJ Foundation, the Helen Bader Foundation, the Fleck Foundation, the Baur Foundation, the Q3 Company, the American

Education Reform Council, the Kern Family Foundation, Edison Schools, the Annie E. Casey Foundation, the Challenge Foundation, Mosaica Education, the Princeton Review, the Olin Foundation, and the Pumpkin Foundation (BAEO Symposia programs, 2001, 2002, 2003; BAEO website). Within BAEO's first year of existence, such donations enabled the organization to spend an estimated $3 million on advertisements promoting vouchers in Milwaukee, Washington, D.C., Cleveland, and Florida (PFAW, 2001).

Aside from its funders, there are various groups and individuals that BAEO names as its allies in promoting educational options for low-income families, and it is to these that I now turn. My intention is not just to identify BAEO's allies, but also to map out the overlaps and tensions in educational agendas that exist between BAEO and these other pro-voucher forces. As Kaleem Caire, BAEO's former executive, has noted, there have been significant instances when BAEO has parted ways with other coalition members over specific dimensions of the educational "choice" debate. For example, BAEO has only supported vouchers for low-income parents in particular urban contexts. In voucher mobilizations in California and Michigan, in which vouchers were targeted more universally (e.g., without regard to family income), or to urban districts that BAEO did not feel were "ripe" for vouchers, BAEO has refused to offer its endorsement (Caire interview, March 5, 2001). Similarly, BAEO has parted ways with organizations with which it is otherwise allied over the issue of tuition tax credits, as these are typically targeted to middle-income and wealthier families, and not just working-class and poor families. In sum, according to Caire, BAEO is not committed to educational free markets as a first principle. Rather, it believes that certain aspects of market dynamics can be harnessed for the purpose of bringing about social justice for some marginalized communities. In this regard, it differs significantly from free market fundamentalists such as the Rose and Milton Friedman Foundation and the Mackinac Center for Public Policy (phone conversation with Caire, February 25, 2001).

Table 4.1 illustrates the coalitions around voucher expansion in Milwaukee. The left column lists organizations with which BAEO considers itself to be allied, and the right column lists those organizations that BAEO would identify as its opposition. Although I will concentrate on BAEO's allies, I include opponents in order to later open a discussion about possible and actual points of articulation between BAEO and orga-

Table 4.1 The Coalitions around Voucher Expansion in Milwaukee

Voucher Expansion Advocates, Selected	Voucher Expansion Opponents, Selected
Bradley Foundation	National Education Association (NEA)
Kern Family Foundation	American Federation of Teachers (AFT)
Walton Foundation	Urban League
Helen Bader Foundation	National Association for the Advancement of
Rose and Milton Friedman Foundation	Colored People (NAACP)
Fleck Foundation	Most Milwaukee Black leaders (post 1995)
Olin Foundation	State Representative Polly Williams (D)
Golden Rule Insurance Company	Most civil rights organizations
Hudson Institute	People for the American Way (PFAW)
Heritage Foundation	American Civil Liberties Unions (ACLU)
Public Policy Forum	American Jewish Conference
Reason Foundation	Most Democrats
Institute for Justice	Rethinking Schools
Landmark Institute	Center for Education Research, Analysis, and
Parents Acquiring Choice in Education (PACE)	Innovation (CERAI)
Empowering Parents for Informed Choices (EPIC)	[Public] school-based organizations
American Education Reform Council (AERC)	State school boards
Black Alliance for Educational Options (BAEO)	State departments of education
Partners Advancing Values in Education (PAVE)	
Center for Education Reform	
Black America's Political Action Committee (BAMPAC)	
Milwaukee Mayor John Norquist (D)	
Most Republicans	
Ex-Wisconsin Governor Tommy Thompson (R)	
Metro Milwaukee Association of Commerce (MMAC)	
Most religious interest groups	
Catholic Archdiocese	
National Catholic Educators Association (NCEA)	
Private school groups	
Edison Schools, Inc.	
Mosaica, Inc.	
Wisconsin Association of Nonpublic Schools (WANS)	

nizations opposed to voucher expansion (interview with Caire, March 5, 2001; author's field notes from BAEO symposia; BAEO symposia programs 2001, 2002, 2003).

Although Table 4.1 is not intended to be exhaustive—there are certainly other organizations that have weighed in on the debate—it does give us a feeling for the political terrain around vouchers both in Milwaukee and nationally. Shading in the chart indicates various categories of organizations participating in the debate. Under "voucher expansion advocates" are first a variety of foundations, including those discussed earlier in this chapter, that have provided financial and/or ideological support for BAEO's agenda. After that are two organizations, the Landmark Institute and the Institute for Justice, that have primarily provided support in the area of litigation, followed by a group of national organizations that advocate for vouchers, including the American Education Reform Council (AERC), the Black Alliance for Educational Options (BAEO), Partners Advancing Values in Education (PAVE), and the Center for Education Reform. The next grouping is of political organizations and entities that are active in issues beyond education, including Black America's Political Action Committee (BAM-PAC), Milwaukee Democratic Mayor John Norquist, most Republicans, and ex-Wisconsin Republican Governor Tommy Thompson, followed by the Milwaukee business association (the Metro Milwaukee Association of Commerce, or MMAC), religious groups such as the Christian Coalition, the Catholic Archdiocese, the National Catholic Educational Association, and for-profit education providers such as Edison Schools, Inc. and Mosaica, Inc. Finally I list private, non-profit, and non-partisan organizations that are particular to the debate around expanding vouchers in the state of Wisconsin, most notably the Wisconsin Association of Nonpublic Schools (WANS), Parents Acquiring Choice in Education (PACE), and Empowering Parents for Informed Choices (EPIC).

In the right column of Table 4.1, under voucher expansion opponents, we have cataloged by shading: teachers' unions, including the NEA and the AFT, traditional civil rights organizations, such as the Urban League and the National Association for the Advancement of Colored People (NAACP), most Milwaukee Black leaders, including Democratic State Representative Polly Williams, most Democrats, and civil liberties organizations such as the American Civil Liberties Union (ACLU), People for the American Way (PFAW), and the American Jewish Conference. Voucher expansion opponents also include the Milwaukee-based Rethinking Schools collective, the Center for Education Research, Analysis, and Innovation (CERAI), public school-based organizations, state school boards, and state departments of education.

The headings of the two columns are intentionally *not* given as "pro-MPCP" and "anti-MPCP," in that it is significant to recognize that the MPCP is not a single static entity. Rather, it is an entity that, before and since its creation, has responded and changed in accordance with shifting political pressures and trajectories, as will be discussed below. I have also not labeled the organizations "pro-voucher" and "anti-voucher" because there are organizations on both sides of the chart that would shift their allegiance depending on the specific aspects of proposed or actual voucher programs. Rather, I have designed the chart to reflect the relationship between the various organizations and the status quo of the MPCP today. So, for example, State Representative Polly Williams and most Black leaders in Milwaukee today cannot be said to be voucher opponents, as many of these individuals, particularly Representative Williams, were central to the creation of the program in 1990. However, they can be said to be opponents of voucher *expansion*, as shall be discussed below, in that many have expressed their opposition to the 1995 legislation that enabled sectarian schools to enter the program (Witte, 2000). This categorization helps us to visualize the MPCP as the contested dynamic educational terrain that it actually is. Although there are many organizations that, for example, favor the expansion of the program, the direction in which or the degree to which the program should be expanded is something on which they would in all likelihood disagree with each other, sometimes quite sharply.

To help us further understand the MPCP as a contested and dynamic educational terrain, it will be useful to describe the ways in which the parameters of the program have shifted since its inception in 1990. The particular shape the program took at its beginning was itself an object of intense political debate, with some Republican political figures, including then-Wisconsin Governor Tommy Thompson, favoring a much more "universal" (for example, in terms of income qualifications) voucher than Polly Williams and other African American supporters of the legislation were actually willing and able to achieve. Originally, the program was only open to nonsectarian public schools. Private religious schools were not legislated into the program until 1995, and were not able to actually participate in the MPCP until 1998, when the Wisconsin Supreme Court lifted an appeals court injunction predicated on constitutional issues of separation of church and state. Furthermore, although initially MPCP students could only comprise 49% of a participating school's enrollment, this ceiling was lifted to 65% with legislative amendments in 1993, and was eliminated altogether in the 1995 changes. Whereas the 1990 form of the program only allowed students to join the program if they were transferring in from one of the Milwaukee Public Schools or just entering school for the first time, the 1995 legislation allowed students to transfer from other private non-MPCP schools in the city of Milwaukee, as long as these students were at or below the third grade. The total cap on participating students has also gradually been raised, from 1% of the Milwaukee Public Schools population in 1990, to 1.5% in 1993, and to 15,000 total students in 1995. Finally, whereas the initial legislation required that MPCP schools use no admissions criteria, and utilize a process of random selection in cases where an individual school became oversubscribed, the 1993 legislation allowed schools to give preference in admissions to siblings of current attendees (Witte, 2000).

Although all these parameters have shifted, there are two that have not changed as of this writing. Allowable family income for participation is still capped at 175% of federal poverty guidelines, and participating students must reside in the City of Milwaukee.

Table 4.2 demonstrates not only the shifts in the MPCP described above, but also lays out possible more universal directions for the program's expansion in the coming years. The status quo of the program, as of this writing in 2003, is indicated by underlining (Witte, 2000).

Table 4.2 outlines the two significant legislative changes in the MPCP since it was conceived in 1990. Recapping these chronologically, the first legislative modification of the program in 1993 permitted sibling preference in admissions, increased the proportion of MPCP students allowable at a given school to 65%, and raised the ceiling on overall participation to 1.5% of enrollment in Milwaukee Public Schools. The 1995 legislation allowed sectarian schools to enter the program, as long as they were deemed to primarily serve a "secular purpose." The 1995 legislation also admitted students below fourth grade from other private schools in the City of Milwaukee, eliminated the cap on MPCP enrollment in a given school, and raised the total participation limit of the program to 15,000 (Witte, 2000).

The overall momentum of these legislative changes has been to push the initially targeted voucher program increasingly in the direction of universality. Not a single change has been implemented in the program that moves it *away* from universality. The bracketed entries in the table indicate even more universal directions in which the program could be taken in the future.

Table 4.2   Milwaukee Parental Choice Program as a Dynamic Contested Terrain

	←TARGETED —————————————————————————————— UNIVERSAL→		
Selection of students by schools	1990: Random selection →	1993: Sibling preference →	[admissions criteria]
Income caps for receiving voucher	1990: 175% of Federal poverty guidelines →	[increased limits] →	[no limits]
Types of schools that can participate in program	1990: Nonsectarian only →	1995: Sectarian schools join; serve "secular purpose"	
Areas partaking in voucher program	1990: City of Milwaukee only →	[other low-income areas] →	[entire state]
Which children can participate in program	1990: Only from MPS or just entering →	1995: private students below 4th →	[all]
Maximum percent MPCP students in a school	1990: 49 % →	1993: 65 % →	1995: 100 percent
Maximum no. of students using vouchers overall	1990: 1 % of MPS →	1993: 1.5 % of MPS → 1995: 15,000 →	[no limit]

A way to further analyze shifts in the program as represented in the table is to subdivide the parameters of the program between those that are supply-oriented and those that are demand-oriented. Allowing sectarian schools into the program is an expansion on the supply side, as is the lifting of the ceiling on MPCP enrollment as a portion of a school's total enrollment, in that both of these changes increase the number of "seats" in the program. Allowing schools to utilize admissions criteria in selecting students should also be seen as a shift in the supply side, since providing schools with this flexibility in choosing students will draw more cautious schools that have remained on the sidelines in Milwaukee into the program. Finally, a hypothetical expansion of the program beyond the City of Milwaukee could be either a supply-side change or a demand-side change.

It would be a supply-side change if *schools* outside the City of Milwaukee are allowed to participate. It would be on the demand side if *students* outside the City of Milwaukee are allowed to participate.

Other demand-side shifts would include raising or eliminating the cap on income, allowing private students above grade 3 into the program, and raising or eliminating the cap on the total number of students participating in the program.

Different groups within the voucher alliance favor different sorts of shifts, on the supply side as well as the demand side. For example, BAEO currently supports legislation introduced by two Republican state legislators to increase the supply of high schools in the program (which, as noted earlier, are currently quite limited) by allowing private schools throughout Milwaukee County, not just the city, to participate (Carr, 2003). BAEO is also currently working on reform on the demand side, to raise the 15,000 cap on total participation, which it believes will pose an obstacle as early as 2005 (personal communication with Basimah Abdullah, Clara Mohammed School principal).

To demonstrate the contested nature *within the alliance of voucher expansion advocates* of the parameters of the MPCP, we can situate various members of the voucher alliance within the table according to their expressed position on actual and hypothetical expansions of the program. Here is the table again (shown as Table 4.3), but with various expansion advocates (as well as some opponents) inserted into the horizons in italics, in approximation of their indicated positions on the respective issues (Witte, 2000).

Table 4.3 helps us visualize significant tensions within the alliance supporting vouchers in Milwaukee. Some members of the alliance explicitly and publicly reject BAEO's defense of the program as one targeted for low-income urban families. For example, both Mayor Norquist and the Wisconsin Association of Nonpublic Schools (WANS, an umbrella organization of private religious schools, including the Catholic Archdiocese) have called for the removal of income criteria for participation in the program entirely (Witte, 2000, p. 170). The Metropolitan Milwaukee Association of Commerce (MMAC), the Catholic Archdiocese, and other religious groups have opposed random selection in admissions (Witte, 2000, p. 164), arguing that schools should be allowed to set up admissions criteria based on student attributes such as academic performance and personal conduct. Meanwhile, the woman who is considered the mother of school choice, Representative Polly Williams, has complained bitterly,

Table 4.3 Milwaukee Parental Choice Program as a Dynamic Contested Terrain, with the Positions of Various Groups and Individuals Inserted

←TARGETED		UNIVERSAL→
Selection method of students by MPCP schools	1990: Random selection →	1993: Sibling preference → [admissions criteria] Rep. Polly Williams MMAC, Archdiocese, *BAEO* *other religious groups*
Income cap for families receiving voucher	1990: 175% of Federal poverty guidelines → [increased limits] → [no limits] *Rep. Polly* BAEO (once in the program, allow income to *Mayor Norquist* *Williams* marginally exceed, or utilize sliding scale) *WANS*	
Types of schools that can participate in program	1990: Nonsectarian only → 1995: Sectarian schools join; serve "secular purpose" **Rep. Polly Williams, other Black leaders** *Bradley Foundation* **American Jewish Conference** *BAEO*	
Areas partaking in voucher program	1990: City of Milwaukee only → [other low-income areas] → [entire state] *BAEO (allow other schools—but not* *PACE* *students—in Milwaukee County to participate)*	
Which children can participate in program	1990: Only from MPS or just entering → 1995: private students below 4th → [all] *NCEA, **BAEO*** *Governor Thompson*	
Maximum percent of MPCP students in an MPCP school	1990: 49 % → 1993: 65 % → 1995: 100 percent ***BAEO***	
Maximum no. of students using vouchers overall	1990: 1 % of MPS → 1993: 1.5 % of MPS → 1995: 15,000 → [no limit] ***BAEO***	

along with other Black leaders, including Representative Spencer Coggs and Senator Gwendolyn Moore, about the expansion of the MPCP to include religious schools (Witte, 2000, p. 168). According to University of Wisconsin researcher John Witte, the only significant Black political leader in Milwaukee who remains a supporter of the MPCP program is Howard Fuller. He writes, "The coalition supporting that expansion has grown from the core of black supporters representing poor, minority constituents to include the white political, business, and religious community.

The process has marginalized black leaders, many of whom have withdrawn support for the newly formulated program" (Witte, 2000, p. 169).

Although, as noted previously, BAEO now supports the expansion of participating schools to areas of Milwaukee County outside the city, the organization Parents Acquiring Choice in Education (PACE) favors the program's expansion throughout the state. Finally, the National Catholic Educators Association (NCEA) and former Governor Tommy Thompson have supported the inclusion of all children in Milwaukee attending any private school at any grade level (Witte, 2000, pp. 163, 183).

In sum, there are significant tensions not only within BAEO, but also between BAEO and its allies in the voucher coalition. Some of these tensions between African American (as well as Latino) low-income supporters of vouchers and various other constituencies can also be summarized outside the framework of BAEO and the other organizations. For example, some rural and suburban public school parents, despite frequently supporting candidates who endorse vouchers, fear the increased costs that expanded vouchers could represent. Similarly, some non-voucher private school parents are wary of the "problems" that vouchers might bring into "their" schools. Some private school administrators do not want their schools to participate in the MPCP out of fear that their school's mission will be diluted, or that their school might be regulated by an outside authority. Finally, there are real tensions between some voucher expansionists and Black and Latino community leaders who feel that the program should be for urban low-income families (author's fieldnotes, 2001 BAEO Symposium).

The fact that different individuals and groups would occupy different positions along the table's seven horizons corresponding to the program's parameters (selection of students, income cap, etc.) points to the overlaps and tensions within the alliance that were alluded to previously. These tensions and overlaps are very significant, in that they point to the sutures in the alliance that are also the sites of the alliance's greatest instability. The points of suture represent *unmet needs* for the various alliance members involved. Of most value to this study, and as will be discussed in greater detail in this volume's conclusion, these points of suture represent an entry point for progressive modernizers, who may share sympathy with African American voucher advocates over the dire educational circumstances in urban public schools that have motivated their voucher advocacy, but who do not see educational marketization as a means of ameliorating these circumstances.

Having explored tensions and articulations within BAEO at a leadership level and between BAEO and other members of the voucher alliance, I turn in the next chapter to an examination of the discourses of grassroots advocates for and users of the voucher program—African American families who BAEO has helped to connect to larger conservative educational and social forces.

5

SHOPPING AROUND FOR JUSTICE:

ENHANCING THE VALUE OF BLACK CHILDREN IN THE MARKETPLACE

Public school has a lot of changes that I felt that needed to be made. I'm not knocking public schools. Public school has a lot of good things to offer. But public school also on the other hand has a lot of improving to do. And I resented that being African-American—and of course I live in one of the poorer neighborhoods—my children were stigmatized by that. And they felt like they were giving you something. I'm a working mother. I pay taxes. It's like nobody else's. ... And my taxes help pay for public education. So as far as I was concerned, it was a paid education. You know, and I didn't appreciate the stigma like you have to take whatever I give you, you know. It's free. You ain't paying for nothing. And you know, that was the stigma. And it was so hard to get anything done. I was always. ... It was always a fight. And I was looking in search of *something different*.

Sonia Israel, mother of two daughters who attended Mariama Abdullah School

The primary argument of this chapter is that families use vouchers in Milwaukee and become articulated to the otherwise conservative voucher movement as a result of the "elements of good sense" they possess concerning the poor quality of education available to African American children through Milwaukee's public schools. This movement to vouchers, like other historical struggles for quality education on the part of Milwaukee's communities of color, is a product of agency on a terrain not of parents' own choosing.

Parents and guardians exhibit this structurally and discursively limited agency in two related but analytically distinguishable subaltern processes. First, working-class and poor parents and guardians—much like Sonia Israel in the opening quote—respond to the poor material conditions and pathologizing racial discourses found in most urban public schools by acting tactically and "making do" within the educational options that are available to them. In the case of Ms. Israel, this entails "looking in search of something different"—disarticulating oneself from that which is normative and unacceptable, and rearticulating oneself to opportunities that present themselves, such as the MPCP.

The second subaltern process, which frequently "hitches a ride" with the first, is related to identity formation. That is, working-class parents and guardians often "tactically inhabit" circulating discourses and their concomitant subject positions—such as Sonia Israel's *consumer* or *taxpayer*—in order to seize available opportunities and subvert the pejorative racializing discourses that lay claim to them.

Therefore, occasionally we see tandem processes of structural and discursive "poaching" (de Certeau, 1984). In this process of "making do" within both the structural and the discursive educational moments of conservative modernization—inhabiting market-embedded schools as well as market-embedded discourses and their concomitant subject positions—parents and guardians do not necessarily "become conservative" (although this is one possibility). Rather, to invoke de Certeau's phraseology, parents and guardians sometimes "manipulate the mechanisms of discipline and conform to them in order to evade them" (de Certeau, 1984, p. xiv). Following de Certeau, one of my objectives in this chapter is to discern an "anti-discipline" in the "ways of operating" which "constitute the innumerable practices by means of which users reappropriate the space organized by techniques of sociocultural production" (de Certeau, 1984, p. xiv).

In undertaking this, I analyze the more than 200 pages of self-prepared verbatim interview transcripts that constitute the core field data with voucher parents and guardians in this study. I also consult hours of audio tape and field notes from interviews and observations with principals, teachers, and their classrooms at the five participating voucher schools.

Each of the parent/guardian interview transcripts has been coded for four themes related to the core questions of this study. First, I have coded all transcripts for autobiographical information regarding subjects' life histories, as well as their children's scholastic histories. The second category for which I have coded intersects with the autobiographical narratives, but is related more directly to the subject positions and discourses in which parents and guardians participate. That is, I have coded instances in which the interviewed parent or guardian adopts, subverts, or resists particular educational and social discourses and subject positions. Next, I have coded subjects' remarks on the positive and negative attributes of chosen voucher schools and the MPCP in general. Finally, I have catalogued comments from parents and guardians that reveal their perspectives on public schools attended by their children and Milwaukee Public Schools in general.

In what follows, I present the remarks of parents and guardians regarding both Milwaukee Public Schools and MPCP schools "at face value."[1] That is, my purpose in this research is not to discern whether the schools and the programs actually function and perform the way the parents and guardians in this study say they do. (In fact, during my field observations and interviews with personnel at the five schools it became clear to me that, although characteristics of a few of the schools seemed to match my interview subjects' portrayals fairly well, others most certainly did not.) My purpose in this research is also not to evaluate the schools in the study vis-à-vis interview subjects' expressed expectations. Instead, as discussed above, I am primarily interested in the consciousness, ideological processes, and identity formation that are in motion as parents and guardians navigate their choices within Milwaukee's "educational market." Because I present their remarks at face value, and because my interview subjects were, with one exception, hand-picked by MPCP school administrators, we can expect their comments regarding their chosen schools to be very positive. Conversely, their comments about schools they've rejected can be expected to be quite negative.

Although this approach doesn't necessarily give us reliable information about the various Milwaukee public schools and MPCP schools interview subjects discuss, it does give us a fairly good sense—albeit a co-constructed one, as discussed in the appendix on research methods—of the interview subjects' ideological formation and identity processes in Milwaukee. This in turn helps clarify why voucher families choose particular schools while rejecting others. Even more importantly, it reveals how and in what ways they become articulated into conservative educational movements.

In the presentation and analysis of fieldwork that follows, all names of individuals, schools, neighborhoods, and other explicitly identifying factors in the data have been altered. This is undertaken in compliance with research ethics and protocol that require that every reasonable measure be taken to protect individual and institutional identities from harm.

Mariama Abdullah School

Mariama Abdullah is a private independent Islamic school with a 30-year history on Milwaukee's north side. Although the school has offered a curriculum rooted in Qu'ranic perspectives to families in the neighborhood for more than a generation, it did not become financially accessible to most in the community until 1998, when the Wisconsin Supreme Court lifted an injunction prohibiting sectarian schools from participating in the MPCP.

Mariama Abdullah School is situated in a rather modest setting. The only marked entrance to the school building—housed in a converted leather factory—is through a corner storefront abutting a liquor store adorned in gaudy electric signs. When I first visited the school, about a month into the new school year, the storefront windows were boarded up and the building was largely surrounded by scaffolding, due, I soon learned, to extensive renovations and improvements. Today, although some classrooms remain without windows, many are bright and sunny. Additionally, a large space has been created in the rear of the building for daily prayer, assemblies, and cafeteria service.

Mariama Abdullah School offers four-year-old kindergarten through tenth grade, although most of the school's 105 students are concentrated at the elementary level. Nearly all subscribing families use an MPCP voucher to meet the school's tuition. Eighty-six percent of the enrolled students are African American, and 4% are Asian (and mostly Muslim). Fifty-six percent are female. The average class size at the school is 10, and there are 10 regular teachers. No services are offered for students with physical disabilities or moderate to high learning disabilities.

In accordance with its Muslim mission, the school provides daily prayer services and optional Qu'ranic study. Girls must wear headscarves at all times. The school's motto is, "Ensuring the right to think for ourselves."

Mariama Abdullah's principal and staff were unique among the five participating schools in extending access to precisely the types of parents and guardians I was most interested in locating. That is, school personnel went out of their way to accommodate my request to speak with one parent who was new to the school, one parent who was a more established member of the school community, and one parent who had elected to leave the school. The school's responsiveness to this final request was particularly noteworthy, especially because school staff had not yet been able to ascertain why the parent had pulled her two daughters from the school. Other schools in the study were much more cautious in the access that they allowed to parents and guardians.

Alexis Turner

Alexis Turner is the mother of two boys attending Mariama Abdullah. One is a seventh grader, and the other is in third grade. Neither child has attended any other school. Because the school was not able to accept MPCP vouchers until 1998 because of its sectarian nature, Ms. Turner initially utilized a privately funded voucher from the Bradley-financed Partners Advancing Values in Education (PAVE), which paid half her older son's tuition.

Ms. Turner now works as a secretary at the school. Because of this, she is able to offer insight about the school's culture both as an everyday "insider" and as a long-time parent.

Like many low-income single parents, this is not Ms. Turner's only paid employment. Her second job involves supervising visitations for parents who have been separated by the state from their children. Despite working two jobs, Ms. Turner does not feel she has reached the middle class. As a mother who has struggled considerably to make ends meet for her children, she is angered by the assumptions many more privileged families make about the lives of low-income urban residents:

> You can be low-class people and still have morals. ... You know, some people don't think that. They just think, "Oh! You're all ... everybody's on welfare, all the men are in jail." That is not true. You know, you do have working class people that just are low-income people, that is still stable. You know, just because I don't drive this kind of car and that kind of car, don't mean that I'm not ... I don't have the same feelings and values that you have.

In order to protect the access to private schools that she and other low-income mothers in Milwaukee now possess, Ms. Turner has become politically involved in efforts to shield the MPCP from legislative and judicial threat. She joined busloads of other voucher supporters in the summer of 2001 as they petitioned state legislators at the state capital in Madison.

In part, Ms. Turner chose Mariama Abdullah over other private MPCP schools because it serves the types of families with which she strongly identifies. She intentionally avoided schools considered to be more prestigious, or which are thought to offer higher status to their attendees.

> I don't want my kid to be like that. You know, I don't want my kid even to be around that. So, I would rather for my kid to go to this school over here that you might consider to be low-income, and be around realistic people that's going to get the bigger picture, than to be over here with people, who, you know, are looking at you, down on you, because, "You're only here because of Choice."

Ms. Turner also appreciates the sense of family she finds at Mariama Abdullah, which is reflected in the close relationship the school has forged, even in curriculum, with the community in which it is embedded. Although her family is not Muslim (the paternal grandfather of the children is a practicing Muslim), Turner applauds the ethical and moral focus that structures everyday school life.

> I tell them all religions are the same. All religions you can get something from. ... I teach them that any religion has their good points ... they teach about morals, values. Even though they're teaching it from the Qu'ran ... they're learning about God, you know that it is a higher power. ... They keep them in that frame of mind when they're here. And then throughout the day, they're reminded of it.

But the Qu'ran-based moral curriculum is not the primary draw for Ms. Turner.

> I like the size of the school. ... I like that everybody just knows about ... everyone. It's a close-knit family. Problems get solved quicker, I believe. ... The sizes of the classes are small. ... They teach them pride within their self, who they are—to be proud of who they are.

In contrast, Ms. Turner finds public schools woefully out of touch with and disparaging of students' life worlds. And she blames teacher preparation programs for failing to provide teachers, who typically come from privileged backgrounds, with the ability and the insight to see their students through other than a normative middle-class lens.

If you're going to be a teacher today, I think they need to totally change the whole curriculum of teaching, reaching these kids. Because the way it's done today is not reaching them. You've got a high drop out rate. Kids don't want to go to school for whatever reason, and I think it's not just the parents. ... A lot of the teachers are not equipped to deal with the kids now. ... Kids are coming from broken homes. ... The two parents might be in jail. You have the grandparents raising the kids, which can't deal with the issues, or ... have their own issues. ... So the teacher has to be taught how to deal with these issues that these kids are bringing to school. And if you're in the mind-frame that no matter what color you are ... If you come from a middle-class family—you've never struggled, you've never dealt with these issues—you're not going to be able to reach these kids. ... A lot of people think life is gravy and it's all good. "Well, I don't see what the problem is. They got the chances just like me." ... They don't want to open their eyes to see it's a lot of issues that you don't even know about. ... These kids have been through things that—I'm 37, have never seen. Abused mentally and physically. How can you reach that kid that's coming to school in a class every day with all of these issues on their mind? It's no way that that kid is going to function like a normal kid. And then it's like, "Well, he's behind grade level." Of course he's going to be!

The problem, according to Ms. Turner, isn't just that public schools hire teachers unprepared to see students as situated beings. They also enact disciplinary policies oriented more to the short-term interests of teachers and administrators than those of low-income families. Ms. Turner illustrates this point with a story about her niece, enrolled at a public middle school. "She got suspended like every week." When Ms. Turner, whose sister was unavailable, met with the school's principal with the intention of constructively addressing her niece's behavior, she discovered the girl had already been written off by her teachers as a "problem child" with a dysfunctional "home life." With the school faculty largely uncooperative and unhelpful, Ms. Turner set off on her own to salvage her niece's imploding scholastic career.

Ms. Turner's first move was to pull the rug out from under the pathological labels that were being attached to her niece. "We had her tested. She was at her level. Nothing was wrong with her, or with her learning. The home life was good." Once she had derailed the triumvirate of normative discourses typically framing Black schoolchildren—psychological, mental, and familial dysfunction—Ms. Turner finally "got to the bottom of it." Her niece was deeply angry and depressed about the fact that she needed to live with her grandmother while her mother searched for work in another city. The niece would have to remain in Milwaukee until her mother's employment status would allow the rest of the family to join her.

It is precisely life circumstances such as this that Ms. Turner has in mind when she laments the lack of familiarity most school teachers have with urban students' everyday realities. "You're not helping. Suspending her was not the issue." Because of her work supervising visitations, Ms. Turner also knows that many Milwaukee schoolchildren do not have an empowered adult available to fend off the damage brought about by school practices rooted in normative frames that do not fit students' circumstances or needs.

Furthermore, according to Ms. Turner, the very forms that disciplinary actions take are mismatched to urban students' lives. Suspensions presume a family in which an adult is available at home to supervise the errant child. Not only is this no longer true for most suburban middle-class families, in which all adults in the household typically hold jobs, but it has never been true for most urban low-income families. Although suspensions can temporarily solve individual teachers' problems by removing students with whom they are not able to cope, such disciplinary forms can prove devastating to urban families. For them, a suspension either means that an adult has to take leave from a financially vital job, or the child remains unsupervised.

Turner says teachers and administrators at Mariama Abdullah are more connected to the lives of their parents.

> If a kid gets in trouble … [we] have them do squats, or push ups. They might walk around with the clean-up guy, and they can do chores and stuff like that. Not suspending them. You know, you have to really do something to really get suspended. It's like, because we know that 95% of these kids here are low-income kids. And we know that parent's job is valuable. We know that parent can't just get up and leave. Because we know they need all their money from their job. Nine out of ten they're underpaid, you know. So one day off their check is going to be vital.

Not only are the school's disciplinary measures better suited to the needs and interests of its families, but characteristics of the school yield greater success in preventing the need for more severe forms of punishment. "Here, you can nip it in the bud, before it goes too far, you know." Instead of being allowed to escalate, "at a school like this, it would probably be recognized quicker, too. Because it's a smaller class, so you know— you can see it." Unlike public schools, where Ms. Turner says teachers in larger classrooms are overwhelmed by the number of kids who have problems needing attention, "you have teachers that recognize, something's not right here. Something's going on with this kid. And nine out of ten, we know the parent, because it's a small school."

Even though Ms. Turner feels that vouchers have proved to be a tremendous benefit to her two children, her position as a school secretary has also made her aware of the drawbacks that participation in the MPCP brings for some schools. At the same time that vouchers have been a salvation for financially precarious schools, they also pressure private schools in ways that threaten the core mission around which they were originally formed. This is particularly true for small schools serving predominantly low-income populations. Market pressures impel such schools to join the MPCP with both a "carrot" and a "stick." The "carrot" comes in the form of additional tuition that a school will be eligible to receive if it accepts MPCP students. The "stick," as Turner explained, is the realization that a decision not to participate in MPCP might mean that the school will lose many of those already attending, as low-income families opt to move their children to schools that do accept vouchers.

Yet when small private schools decide to accept vouchers, the mission or ethos that has united the school can become endangered. According to Turner,

> When my son first started, it was the greater population of kids were Muslim. ... Now that Choice has been implemented, you get a variety of kids. So you're getting kids that ... it's not any religion that's not been taught at home. ... They're just picking this school ... because they waited too late for Milwaukee Public Schools. ... Because now we're getting kids that are like problem kids that somebody else didn't want. ... So it opened the doors for a lot of, you know ... people don't see it as a Muslim school no more. They're just seeing it as a school that they chose.

At the same time that Ms. Turner is critical of the motivations some parents have for enrolling their children in Mariama Abdullah, she also sympathizes with the difficulty many parents face in effectively advocating for their children's educational interests.

> [Parents] are struggling. That's right, they have their own ... so, even though they want to come and help, but it's like their battles, it's just so overwhelming that they don't have that extra energy to come see what the problem is. You know ... the husband is in jail now, so now she has these four kids, she's got to work out on her own and ... you've got maybe the high school kid that's skipping school, you got this kid that you need to take to the doctor but you can't because you've got to go to the school. You don't have a car. You know, your income is the problem. You've got the light bill that they're sending you mail saying that it's going to get cut off. You know, so you're overwhelmed with all these different issues that the kid gets lost.

For Ms. Turner, working-class parents face nearly insurmountable challenges that can impede their ability to ensure that their children are receiving a quality education. The fact that families are frequently overwhelmed both inhibits their capacity to act as effective consumers of education and compromises their ability to act as the kind of involved parents that schools increasingly demand.

Sonia Israel

I became interested in interviewing Sonia Israel after reading her positive comments about Mariamma Abdullah School in a Milwaukee newspaper article. In my first meeting with the school's principal I was surprised to learn that, since the time the article had been written, Ms. Israel had withdrawn her two adolescent children from the school. Still, Mariama Abdullah's principal provided me with contact information so that Israel could be included in the study.

Ms. Israel was born in Milwaukee into a Muslim family, and as a young girl attended Mariama Abdullah School along with her sisters and brothers. "[We] were one of the first sets of students there." While this would have been Ms. Israel's first choice for her own children, financial limitations initially prevented her daughters from attending their mother's alma mater. Instead, they first entered public schools.

As is evident in the quote which opened this chapter, Ms. Israel is intensely critical of most Milwaukee public schools. She utilizes poignant metaphors to describe the prospect of her children being assigned to public schools that she did not choose.

> Public Schools, you can't even talk about what they're doing there. Values are just not enforced there. And that's frightening. ... It's like sending your babies in the woods, and you know there's wolves out there. And you really don't have no way—they have to go—and you really don't have any way to really protect them from these wolves, and if somebody gave you an alternative ... "Oh. You don't have to send them out there with these wolves, send them here." You know, you're going to jump on it.

Ms. Israel traces problems she sees in public schools partly to the immense size of the school system. "This huge system, it's kind of hard I guess [for teachers] to come together on something. You know, it's a lot of fighting, a lot of division." Ms. Israel also faults school-level administrators for the lack of unity, and expresses sympathy for embattled teachers.

> The public school system really needs to work with their teachers. I understand teaching is not an easy thing to do, and with these children, they're different from when we grew up. They're not the easiest people to teach anymore. And I understand that. But I think they really need to work together. Their attitudes need to change, they need to start writing up different policies. ... They don't pay our teachers enough. You know, and you have ... let's be honest. You come to work every day and get beat down by the administration, by the kids, by the parents, and your check is 30 ... all you're bringing home is what, 30 grand a year? That's frustrating! So, you know, of course you get a attitude, "Oh, the hell with it!" Just don't come to work, because it's not worth it. It's easy to do that. So I understand that.

However, Ms. Israel does not possess the same sympathy for teachers unions.

> Teachers unions I guess benefits the teacher. But I really think somebody needs to watch over them. Really, I've seen some teachers get away with some stuff ... because of the union. ... They should have been automatically fired, never to return to the educational system.

Ms. Israel finds such protection by teachers unions comparable to the Catholic Church's alleged covering up of sexual molestation on the part of priests. "It really hurt me to hear that those people were betrayed by their priests, and nothing was done. But yeah, that's basically what the union is like."

Although her children started out in public schools, the 1998 Wisconsin Supreme Court ruling enabled Ms. Israel to remove her daughters from a school atmosphere of racial stigma and unresponsiveness and enroll them in the school she most desired. For Ms. Israel, Mariama Abdullah School "is just what they call a temple of my familiar. ... I felt comfortable with it." This comfort was augmented by the fact that, at Mariama Abdullah, "The rate of teen pregnancy, drugs, you know, all of the things that ... the scary things that go on in our public school system, that was one of the things that I know I didn't have to worry about." Ms. Israel credits this reduced incidence to Mariama Abdullah's small size and values-oriented mission.

> It's so easy to be influenced [at the school]. And it's small. It's easy to keep up with everybody. And the basis of it, you know the whole basis of it ... the concept behind the schools is to live ... not just as a Muslim, but like a Catholic school, you know, most rules are based on the Ten Commandments, and they were ... it was values there, and they were enforced.

Furthermore, Ms. Israel generally favors private schools because, "the teachers and the administrators and the principal came together. They supported each other." With smaller class sizes, teachers "could take individuals, and you understood, you know that this one's a little different. I'm going to try this with this one. And this one, I'm going to try this and this. ... You could identify who needed what in the private school system."

However, despite her initial satisfaction, Ms. Israel eventually pulled her children from Mariama Abdullah, in large part because of shortcomings in the school facility that she felt administrators were not addressing.

> They didn't have the facilities that properly accommodated growing girls. That was my issue. And I had struggled with it for about a year ... and the situation had never changed. ... They didn't have those dividers in the bathroom. I was even concerned about the sunlight, especially when dealing with education. I believe for a healthy classroom environment you need windows.

Since withdrawing from Mariama Abdullah School a year ago, Ms. Israel's daughters have been attending sixth and eighth grade, respectively, at a public middle school, at least for the time being. "It takes time to research and find a school. And so they had to go to school by law. So that's where they're at now. ... It's close to my house. At the present time, I don't have any real complaints about it, but we're talking public school. I know what's coming."

Ms. Israel feels that pressures from the voucher system have forced the public schools to at least take notice of the disaffection represented by parental attrition to MPCP schools. "I thank God for Choice, because it's checked the public school system." Yet, although the MPCP has brought about competitive dynamics that she feels are systemically beneficial, there are also aspects of the program that worry her deeply.

> Public school has its pros and cons. So does Choice. And I'm also disappointed in some of these Mom and Pop schools that are popping up, taking advantage of the Choice program. ... They'll paint a house and call it ... Tom Jones Academy ... and write up the proposal, and whatever the guidelines that the state says, you need to do this, to get Choice money, they'll put on that piece of paper ... and boom, that's it.

Thus, although Ms. Israel endorses certain aspects of a market model, she does not believe in the self-regulating properties of markets that neoliberals celebrate.

> You've got these people who are using these children for these vouchers, pocketing it and not properly giving them the proper books, the proper facilities. And they'll take a house or a building or whatever, and they'll call it ... put a name on it ... and get everybody signed up to come there and want teachers... because some of the teachers are not even certified ... and are not even capable of properly teaching those children. ... And I truly believe ... that the Choice program should be regulated ... they should have the department, in the state ... where the Choice program have people come out and regulate those schools. Just don't let anybody come in here ... and you know, hiring teachers in there who don't have education.

Whereas in neoliberal models, poor schools soon cease to exist as a result of their inability to attract or maintain customers, Ms. Israel calls for the regulation of MPCP schools by state government.

Darla Kelly

Darla Kelly is a new parent at Mariama Abdullah. Her son Donald, in sixth grade this year, transferred from another sectarian school participating in the MPCP. Her son spent only one year in Milwaukee Public Schools, as a kindergartner. "I didn't feel that they were educating my son well enough … he didn't have a very good teacher I felt. … And he ended up falling behind." Like many other voucher parents in Milwaukee, Ms. Kelly primarily attributes public school teachers' difficulties to overcrowded conditions.

I think that most teachers would be better teachers if they had smaller classes, if they didn't have so many kids. Because it's just … you know children—they learn differently, they understand differently. You can't have 27 to 30 kids in a classroom, because you can't give them the individual attention that they need.

After the public school, Donald attended a private Lutheran school participating in the voucher program. "Someone had recommended it to me. Their daughter who my son is good friends with went there, and they had gotten positive results out of that school." However, soon after transferring her son, Ms. Kelly began to become disillusioned with the school. She did not find many of the positive attributes touted by the acquaintance who had recommended the school.

Well, I really wasn't ever satisfied with the school, but I figured I would just give them a chance. I didn't just want to take him out after 1 year. The first year I didn't really like the teacher, the second year it was a much better teacher and she worked with him. However, the third, he had a very weak teacher that, I don't know if she has some emotional, or some physical health issues—she was off a lot.

In addition to absenteeism, Ms. Kelly attributes teacher weaknesses at the Lutheran school to racial dynamics. "The school was a predominantly White school, and there was only a couple of Black kids there, and those that were there, they seemed to be a sore thumb apparently. And I didn't really like … I didn't like how they treated [Donald]." Initially, when such racial dynamics first began to manifest themselves, Ms. Kelly downplayed them—particularly to her son.

I don't think he could tell that that's what it was, because I don't raise him to believe in that. So as something happened, and I felt it was racially motivated, he wouldn't necessarily know. He would just tell me. And then a friend of mine … brought her son over there. … And her son actually is a lot darker than [Donald], and he was always … he never had problems [before this], but as soon as he got there, it was like, he was this horrible kid, and I thought, you know I thought I was imagining this, but …

Beyond these troublesome racial dynamics, Ms. Kelly also became frustrated by the fact that the school's all-White teachers presided over classrooms that were just as crowded as many public school classrooms—26 in Donald's final year. Echoing the sentiments of Sonia Israel, Ms. Kelly explained, "I wanted more for my property tax dollars."

Ms. Kelly was subsequently attracted to Mariama Abdullah School by her positive interactions with the school's charismatic principal. "I would have to say that it was just … her personality, and her children." She explained, "I had met them, they were very well-mannered, they didn't speak a lot of slang, they weren't yelling. And she was just talking that there was a couple of male teachers over here, that the class sizes were smaller. And she said, 'Oh! We'll work with him. We'll work with him.'"

Furthermore, a friend of Ms. Kelly "had stated that the test scores here were kind of high, higher than the others, that they had a really good track record in a lot of the academic Olympics, and it sounded like it was good."

Contrary to the racialized manner in which she feels her child was treated at the Lutheran school, "Here, he's just another one of the kids." Not only is her child no longer racially stigmatized, but Kelly feels that as a parent she is no longer dismissed as she had been at the Lutheran school. Ms. Kelly remarked to me that she saw her participation in this study as further evidence of the dignity Mariama Abdullah School accords her as a parent. "[The Principal] calling me asking me to speak to you, that would have never happened at [the Lutheran school]. They would never … they looked at me as 'that Black woman.'"

Ms. Kelly also offered a broad critique of public schools, particularly in regard to their teachers. "I think they have a lot of problems with their teachers, and they're all union, and it's really hard to get rid of a bad teacher in a public school." But she also found private schools to be overly protective of poor teachers. During the time that she first became aware of what appeared to be destructive racial dynamics at the Lutheran school, she explains, "I had went to the principal … and said, 'I don't really think she's a very good teacher.'" The response she received was, "Oh, you're just over-reacting. Give it time." According to Kelly,

The more time you gave it, the further behind ... The entire class was
so far behind because she really wasn't doing a good job. And that's not
fair to any child. ... She had actually been at that school for 23, 24 years.
Just because someone has been doing something for 23, 24 years doesn't
mean that they've been doing it right.

Strikingly, Ms. Kelly criticizes school teachers by inverting the frames
of pathology typically reserved for Black schoolchildren, turning them
back onto the teachers themselves. "They don't seem to be too much on
the right track to me, they seem to be a little out of touch or something.
I really don't know." When asked what it was that they were out of touch
with, Ms. Kelly responded, "With reality." She continued, "Just ... they
seem to be *wild*. And very *loose*. And that's not what I send my child to
school for, *or what I expect my child to be involved in* [emphasis added]."
Kelly casts back onto teachers the very qualities with which Black schoolchildren are frequently denigrated. For her, it's not the Black boys but
rather the Lutheran school teachers who are "wild." And public school
teachers, not young women of color, are derided as "loose." Furthermore,
Ms. Kelly doesn't want her good kid to "get involved in" whatever the
wrong kind of people—the teachers—are up to.

Not only does Ms. Kelly invert discourses of pathology back onto
teachers, she also offers an interesting rearticulation of managerialist
notions of accountability, although here it's possible the co-optation is
less intentional.

I think there's more accountability in a smaller school. That if a child is
like here—there's only 11, 9 or 11 kids in [Donald's] class. If [Donald]
is falling behind, I think there's more accountability towards *the teacher*,
that you know that there's something going on. *You're* not contacting
the parent. *You're* not directing him or educating him in the way that is
best for him. He doesn't have some sort of issues that are holding him
back, so ...

Not only does small class size lead to accountability, but, as Ms. Kelly's
"some sort of issues" implies, it also prevents incompetent teachers from
using normative and racialized assertions about a child, or claims of being
overwhelmed by large class size, as cover for their own shortcomings.

Finally, Ms. Kelly rejects the notion that urban kids should learn values
in school settings, a hallmark of neoconservative educational mobilizations.

"I don't send my child to school for values. That's what's instilled in my child at home. My child comes to school for an education."

Saint Urbina Catholic High School

Saint Urbina, which identifies itself as a "multicultural immersion school" for young women, has played a role in educating children living in Milwaukee's urban core for half a century. The school currently serves 325 young women in grades 9 through 12, of whom 60% receive vouchers through the MPCP. According to its mission statement, the school is committed "to maintaining diversity in ethnic, religious, cultural and economic backgrounds of students." Today, the racial and ethnic makeup of the school is 33% European-American, 27% Latina, 26% African American, 6% Southeast Asian-American, 5% Middle Eastern-American, 2% Native American, and 5% multiethnic, multicultural, and/or multinational.

From a religious perspective, the school's composition is reported as 62% Catholic and 38% non-Catholic. Although the school bases its curriculum in Catholic teachings, it also maintains, according to its website, a strong commitment to Gardner's theory of Multiple Intelligences in curriculum, pedagogy, and evaluation. Furthermore, St. Urbina emphasizes college preparatory and business preparatory educational tracks. Ninety-one percent of the school's young women enter college.

Saint Urbina is a "flagship" school for the MPCP, and its classrooms, students, and parents frequently receive sharply positive attention in promotional materials, as well as news coverage about the program. Perhaps more so than any other MPCP school, St. Urbina is held to represent the voucher program at its very best.

However, the school has been lavished not just with praise by the program's promoters and evaluators, it has also been lavished with grants by at least 35 different corporate, private, and nonprofit foundations and contributors. Between 1996 and 2001, St. Urbina received four grants from the Bradley Foundation totaling $200,000 (Media Transparency, 2003). Although the amount of each of these four gifts from Bradley, taken individually, is only equivalent to roughly 2% of the school's annual operating budget, nevertheless the grants have been targeted for projects (e.g., for the renovation of the school's science labs) that have made an indelible contribution to the school's overall appeal (Media Transparency, 2003). Although such generosity should be lauded for the benefit it brings to the school's students, it nevertheless undermines neoliberal arguments that schools like St. Urbina can be easily and widely replicated, and that market forces alone are enough to impel other schools to follow St. Urbina's example. That our inner-city schools need infusions of capital in order to more effectively serve their students is the argument of those on the educational left, and not typically that of dominant groups within conservative modernization.

Dasha Dapedako

Dasha Dapedako is an award-winning jazz vocalist, a renowned African storyteller, and a paraprofessional fifth grade reading teacher at a Milwaukee Public Schools elementary school. Her daughter, Namiya, is a high school senior at St. Urbina, in which she enrolled as a ninth grader after attending public schools at both the elementary and middle school levels. Although Namiya had not wanted to attend the all-girls Catholic School, preferring instead the more social environment of the public school that her friends would attend, Ms. Dapedako insisted on St. Urbina. Enabled by the recent availability of vouchers for sectarian school attendance, Ms. Dapedako removed her daughter from a school where she felt her daughter was likely to affiliate with people who were not positive influences. "I think [St. Urbina's] really saved her, because she's the kind of kid that's easily led."

However, Ms. Dapedako believes that quality options are occasionally available in the public schools, as evidenced by her son's enrollment in a performing arts magnet school. Yet she felt her daughter faced too many social distractions in a co-ed school environment, and worried that public school teachers would not keep her apprised of her daughter's performance, "because they don't always return parents' calls." Primarily, what creates such concerns for Ms. Dapedako is size. "It's too many kids. It's just too many kids in one building. ... And the class sizes, unless they're on SAGE in the lower grades, the class sizes average 26, 27, 28, 29. That's a lot to handle. I mean it's just ... it's too much. ... And anything over 20 is too much. Fifteen is ideal." Ms. Dapedako offers this as an insider to public schools, given her position as an elementary public school educational assistant.

> And so that's one of the problems in the public school, because what that leaves the teachers is during most of the time, so much of our time is spent in discipline, that it's probably half and half. We probably spend

half the time in discipline, so then you get *curriculum* that is designed to help in discipline.

For Ms. Dapedako, the problems in public schools related to class size are compounded by the distance most children must travel to their schools. She is nostalgic for the way in which she remembers schools as rooted in their respective neighborhoods.

> When we were kids our school was within walking distance. We could go home for lunch, and everybody, Miss So-and-So saw you on the way home and Miss So-and-So was watching you. If she saw you hanging with the wrong kids, she'd call your mama: "You know, she was out there with so and so and so and so the other day." And you'd come, your mom would say, "What you doing walking with so-and-so?" You know? And you had a better network of watchers, and people that would keep you on track.

Today, "Children come from all over the city. You know, it's some-thing different when you know your mom and dad are just a couple of blocks away." Even though Ms. Dapedako lives more than 5 miles from her daughter's school, she feels that smaller class sizes at St. Urbina relieve some of the pressures posed by this distance. "With the smaller class size, even if kids live outside of the neighborhood of the school, it becomes a neighborhood because of that smaller class size. And the parents and the kids, the teachers can have a much easier time keeping up with each other."

Besides offering substantially smaller class sizes, Ms. Dapedako was attracted to St. Urbina's by a host of other qualities.

> I needed to put [Namiya] in a more private, more closed, guided envi-ronment. Because she needed a lot more supervision than public school would have provided on a social level. ... And it worked, because at [St. Urbina's] she didn't have to worry about competing with the boys, or competing for the boys. So it left her the whole time to be totally involved in her academics, and she took to it like water. And she's a performer, so there were a lot of performing opportunities through [St. Urbina] also.

According to Ms. Dapedako, most public schools in Milwaukee suffer from cultural and socioeconomic homogeneity. "You have mostly kids that come from the same cultural base, same economic base, and you know the same modern slang teenagers. And that's the paradigm in front of them and that's what they perpetuate." This is something she feels contrasts markedly with the composition of St. Urbina's student body. Whereas at most public schools, students "don't feel any grounding, don't feel any closeness," at her new school, largely because of this diversity, Namiya has "adopted very quickly a sense of family." At St. Urbina's, the diversity that exists is seen by students and faculty to be a very positive attribute of the school.

> She adopted all the girls as her play sisters—the Arab girls, the Spanish girls. She brought home so many kids of so many different ethnic backgrounds, which was wonderful. And they experienced us, and we experienced them. ... And it was a true exchange. It wasn't just a brush with. I mean, they actually talked about the problems that they had adjusting to this society, and she talked about what it was like being African American. I mean, they actually exchanged and I think that's more value. You couldn't get that out of the book. That kind of experience is had, it's not read.

Ms. Dapedako feels that all parents should be able to enroll their children in schools like St. Urbina. And, in this sense, vouchers in Milwaukee are a necessity, "Because some parents, that have values for their children, goals for their children, could never possibly begin to afford it, and that's not fair." She offers herself as an example of someone who, as a loving, caring, and hard-working parent, has fulfilled her responsibilities within what she sees as a social contract that requires that the state now do its part educationally for her children. "You know, I work really hard. And I pay attention to my kids, I cook from scratch, I don't feed them a lot of junk. I'm attentive to their health and their physical well-being, and mental well-being and emotional well-being. And it's an extraordinary job."

Not only does Ms. Dapedako position herself as the subject of a social contract, but she also identifies herself, and those like her, as citizens for whom the state should play a redistributive role. Particularly her usage of the term "choice" in regard to educational access is quite distant from the concept of choice within market discourses.

> Everybody should have the choice to send their kid to a school of the caliber of [St. Urbina's]. They should all be at that level. And the money should be distributed by the government for that. We shouldn't have to petition everybody else in the world. This should be ... I mean, if the

government can't do anything it should be schooling and medical care. That's like bottom line, wouldn't you say? I mean, that's everybody's right. And it should be quality care on both levels. But we're in a free enterprise system, so there's always the privileged two percent. And so basically, when I saw vouchers, I said, "Well what I would like to see, I would like to see the privileged people have to give up the money to put into the program, instead of robbing the state coffers of taxes. ... It needs to be taken from private industry ... and all the rich folks should take a much greater responsibility for their needs."

Although she is a supporter of the MPCP, her frame of reference as a voucher recipient is as a citizen within a redistributive social welfare state, rather than as a consumer within an educational marketplace. She also locates the potential hazards of the voucher program within critical discourses on race.

[The voucher system] brought into my community the greatest fear—the ... preparing of the talented tenth; that we only take the smart ones and prepare them to matriculate into the mainstream, and the rest of the kids are just ... out there. And 90% of the African American children go to public schools, so my campaign for vouchers is, "Okay, yeah. We need help. And these are ... those schools should be available to those of us who qualify, and can work ... willingly go through the process. But it should be open to everybody."

Because Ms. Dapedako is called upon to teach performing arts throughout the Milwaukee metropolitan area, she is painfully aware of the inequalities that exist among public schools, depending on their geographical and socioeconomic location.

I visit some 22 schools in the Milwaukee area. I mean, I go out to Brookfield, and to Marcy, and to Burleigh, and to Waukesha. And I walk into those carpeted schools—they get lockers, and they get computers, and the sunroofs, and their ... I cry when I come back to the middle city. I'm actually angry.

Because of her work as a reading specialist, Ms. Dapedako is made painfully aware of these inequalities on a daily basis. When I met with her, we spoke in a hallway that was her classroom, occupying three-fifths of the width of the hallway, and separated from similarly situated "classrooms" by bulletin-board style dividers. "I'm angry when I get back here, because … I have to teach in this dingy hallway." In my audio recording of our interview, the background din conveys what teaching conditions in this hallway must typically be like.

> This is where I teach. And you know with people passing by, and kids. … My kids, who are having trouble with language arts, are also demanded to have an extraordinary concentration level that a 10-year-old is not capable of. So I have to spend time yelling at them to be quiet. And I don't mean yelling, but I have to be able to speak with them about things. We should be able to talk. We should be able to you know walk around the room, and investigate the math centers. But I have to stay on them. You know, because … people are in the hallway, we've got to be quiet because we're disturbing library. We've got to be quiet because there's a group down the hall. You've got to be quiet, you've got to be quiet, and then I want to just take them out to the playground and say, "Just run. And scream, and holler, and imagine, and look at the sky."

Ms. Dapedako blames these conditions in part on cutbacks in public school budgets resulting from a shifting of funds to the MPCP, and notes the irony that she is simultaneously a participant in the program and, as she sees it, a victim of its effects. "I mean, our building is substandard, you know, and sometimes there's even non-working bathrooms, and just basic, basic, basic."

Themes of equity in distribution permeate Ms. Dapedako's vision for education for Milwaukee's urban population. "I'd like to see the elementary schools, particularly in the public school system, buoyed up. I'd like to see all the public school system brought up to snuff on the elementary level." Curious about what sort of redistributive discourse Ms. Dapedako would invoke, I asked her *how* she felt they should be brought up.

> Money. More money. New buildings. Extensions. Build more room onto what's existing, and cut out some of the busing. If [kids] went to neighborhood schools, we could cut out a significant amount of busing. We could take the money that we use for busing, put it into the maintenance of schools. We could hire the bus drivers and personnel for aide in schools so that they don't lose their jobs, and they're still involved with kids; still working.

Ms. Dapedako's vision for school reform is not one in which schools improve only after teachers unions are broken and schools are forced to become competitive within an educational marketplace.

I think words like competition don't belong in education, they belong in business. ... Competition? When you're dealing with educating children? And they learn at all different levels? And the challenge in elementary schools is how to teach at all these different levels? Some of them are in foster homes. Some of them are living in shelters, and all of these come to bear as to why they can't learn. I think there's also a terrible shift that the teacher should be held responsible, when we are such into so many things that we can't control, as to why this kid is learning or isn't learning. ... This competition in schools, I think it's a crock. And I think it's a way to shift the burden as well. You know, because folks know they should carry the financial burden for the poor folks, so this is a good way to ... "Well, they don't compete. They're not this type of an organization." Yeah, well, you know ...

Although Ms. Dapedako endorses certain aspects of managerialist governance, she does not endorse neoliberal and neoconservative pressures for a universal curriculum.

I do believe that the school system and the administration and in the spending can be realigned, that they should be possibly more run like a corporation. But when it comes to the curriculum, this is something that each school has to set based on its students. And what we do need is ways to assess what our students need, not in competition with Elm Street, which has a bigger money base than [this school]. I say, how are we going to compete? And it's just a terrible burden on us, because every other memo that we get from our front office is, "We've got to draw these kids or we're going to lose kids, and we'll lose our school." Each school has to look at what they have and teach at the level, or teach according to what our clientele is, our student is. But we still should be able to order the same amount of books, we should still have the same budget.

For Ms. Dapedako, that which would harm a school's children is not, as E. D. Hirsch has argued (Hirsch, 1996), the balkanizing effects of a curriculum rooted in students' life circumstances, but rather a universalized curriculum more guided by imperatives of competition than appropriateness and effectiveness for the population that a school actually serves.

Ms. Dapedako, perhaps because of her vantage point within schools, also has tremendous sympathy for teachers.

Teachers! God! They don't do anything but plan, and their whole life is the school and this ... and trying to figure out ... it's a burnout profession. ... I don't think any teacher in the United States makes enough money. When I hear the corporate head's money ... I just resent it. I really do. If there's any revolution coming in this country, it will be us. Because we work so hard, and we raise their children. We educate their children to a level that they can take over those big businesses, and we still are down here in the dust.

Ms. Dapedako endorses vouchers as a state form of redistributive justice countering these educational inequalities, and not as a market form delivering efficiency through market discipline. Because of this, she also opposes the universalization of vouchers. "I think that defeats the purpose, and if there are people that can afford to educate their children, this is supposed to be for the people that can't afford it. ... I think you should have to qualify financially, because that means the people who really need it get it." Furthermore, removal of funding from the public system through dollars-following-children formulae, as punishment for inefficiency, is antithetical to her educational vision. "We've got to find a way to support the voucher system without de-funding any money out of the public schools, because the public schools already don't have enough money."

For Ms. Dapedako, the need for redistributive justice is also apparent in the lack of supervision of children during "those deadly hours between 4 and 6." Phenomena such as teenage pregnancy are "happening more because all parents have to work, and there's less supervision. And when there's less supervision, then folks do what they naturally do. At 15, it's a natural thing." Increasingly, Ms. Dapedako argues, the necessity for more adults in a household to work longer hours means that, "We ask them to take on our jobs at home while we go to work. ... We ask them to be discriminating long before they have the ability to do that." In the absence of relief from increased work hours, Ms. Dapedako cites the need for more after-school programs, such as the Community Learning Centers that now exist in Milwaukee.

In a similar vein, Ms. Dapedako sees forms of discipline routinely used in public schools, such as suspension, as middle-class forms ill-suited to the interests of children from working-class homes. Because all adults in the household are typically at work, "I think sending them out for suspension is the worst thing that we can do." Instead: "My program is always since the day

I came here, give them a toothbrush and send them to the bathroom, okay? Make them do a horrible job. Clean the dust off the baseboards, or hand them a paintbrush." In fact, at her school, paraprofessionals are heavily relied upon to do double duty monitoring hallways and enforcing discipline.

Finally, Ms. Dapedako appreciates the curriculum flexibility that private schools such as St. Urbina's enjoy. Rather than "having to satisfy the needs of the norm in a school system of 100,000 plus," teachers in many private schools are not bound by a centralized curriculum. "The school can be more community-based and more sensitive to the individual needs of the kids. … And the teachers aren't as … you can reach out. You can just design a curriculum that's more realistic for the school."

Gina Price

Gina Price is a single parent pursuing the first two years of a degree in education through Milwaukee Area Technical College. In addition to her studies, Ms. Price is a teacher in a first grade elementary school. She also works two other part-time jobs—one with the school's after-school program, and the other in security. "It takes a lot of energy."

Ms. Price has two children, a son and a daughter. Her son is a fifth grader attending the public elementary school where she teaches and her daughter has attended St. Urbina since entering high school. Ms. Price worries about her son academically, as he has a reading disability. But the fact that she spends the day in the same building with him facilitates her ability to provide him with oversight and support. This will become considerably more difficult next school year, as he will transfer to a public middle school, and Ms. Price is dependent on the bus system for her own transportation. As a result, Ms. Price is considering giving up at least one of her part-time jobs soon, "Because I'm really trying to focus on my son, because of his reading level."

Her daughter, Patricia, decided to apply to St. Urbina High School while she was still in middle school. Ms. Price agreed with her daughter's decision, but would have also been satisfied with a few public schools that she had been considering.

However, due to overcrowding, Ms. Price feels that public school teachers are often not able to tailor their teaching to individual students' needs. "In the public school … you don't get around to all the children. … [Teachers] can't just say, 'Okay. I know he needs this so I'm going to work with him on that.'"

Ms. Price is also bothered by the move many public school programs have made to investigative forms of math and reading, which she feels are not well suited to students like her son. "You have to learn the basics before you can solve anything."

She also worries about the distractions posed by what she describes as a daily fashion show at public schools. "You see the people with the name brand clothes, and children taking other children's things."

At St. Urbina's, because of uniforms, her daughter doesn't have to contend with such distractions. "Everybody wears the same thing. You don't have to worry about, 'Oh, your mom bought you that, and this is Kmart and this is Wal-Mart.'"

Ms. Price also appreciates the strict discipline and academic seriousness that she feels many private schools are able to enforce because of their ability to use expulsion as a threat. "If you don't pick up that grade point, they'll take you out. ... They'll tell you, they won't put up with that foolishness. ... There's strict rules and strict policies. ... They've had seven people's children get kicked out because of ... retaliating." She is intimately familiar with the ability of MPCP schools to carry out such expulsions, because many of those removed from voucher schools end up in her classroom. "We've got more children coming out of voucher schools, because of behavior. ... We've gotten like at least four to five in our class alone. And then after a while you don't have to wonder about why they're out."

Jan Lincoln

Jan Lincoln's daughter transferred to St. Urbina earlier this year as a tenth grader from a public high school. The decision to enter the all-girls Catholic high school was almost entirely her daughter's own choice.

> It was her choice. She decided that she wasn't learning at [the public high school]. She said she thought it was like kids were too rowdy. And ... the teachers couldn't help everybody, or her thing is they *wouldn't* help. And she was like, the classes were too big, and it was like a fashion show. She couldn't learn, you know, being like, them being into boys, and you know, *she* just decided.

Ms. Lincoln's daughter is determined that she will go to college, and would like to become a lawyer. She initially learned about St. Urbina from her two older cousins, who already attended the school. Once she was enrolled, "her grades came up. She's learning more, she comes home from school, do homework, do projects. I mean it's like, she a whole new person since she had been to [St. Urbina]. I mean, grades came up real extremely high. ... And she had no problem getting up in the morning."

According to Ms. Lincoln, this behavior was in stark contrast to her daughter's year at the public high school. "I left to go to work, like at 5:30 in the morning, and then I called to get them up. She just felt, she had a headache, she ain't going to school. ... So she missed a lot of days of school."

Ms. Lincoln is satisfied that St. Urbina has had much higher expectations of her daughter. "When you miss a day of school, your grades drop. And she's going to school every day. She don't want to get no low grade." Furthermore, "They challenge her, because they're much stricter. They want you to learn. They want you to get good grades. And she see that. She like it."

According to Ms. Lincoln, public schools were not always as poor in serving African American children as she believes they are today. "When I was going to public schools, it wasn't like this now. ... Them teachers didn't play. They'd take you out and call your mama. Your mama come do whatever and send you back to the classroom." In contrast, today, "Some teachers ... they play with kids ... and then when it gets too out of control, then they want to call the parent. Don't wait until they get out of control and then call the parent. Call the parent when it first happens."

Knowledge Ventures Learning Academy

Knowledge Ventures Learning Academy is a vocational and academic high school on Milwaukee's north side. According to its mission statement, Knowledge Ventures specializes in "addressing the educational needs of At Risk Youth, teen parents and Learnfare students."[2] The school gives preference to school-age parents, and has a total enrollment of 208 students, of whom 175 (84%) receive vouchers. The majority of the non-MPCP students are behavioral reassignment students, enrolled at Knowledge Ventures through a contractual agreement with Milwaukee Public Schools. Ninety-seven percent of the school's students are African American, and 58% are female.

Although the school offers a college preparatory track, it also provides vocational courses in cosmetology, home mechanics, day care certification, photography, food service, computing, massage therapy, sewing, and business management.

Samantha Murphy

Samantha Murphy, the mother of two children at Knowledge Ventures, is currently pursuing a degree in human services at Milwaukee Area Technical College. Her long-term career objective is to "start a group home for juveniles whose parents are like in a drug program, or who have been abused." Her two children—an older son who graduated the previous June, and a younger son who is a senior this year—have each spent three years in attendance at Knowledge Ventures.

Ms. Murphy pulled her two teenage sons from public schools when she realized that "them being in a bigger environment wasn't working." Initially her children had attended schools on Milwaukee's south side that Ms. Murphy found fairly satisfactory. But when the family relocated to a near north neighborhood, "They put [them] in a north side school closer to my house, and it was *not* going on." She explains, "Well everybody knows that the funding for north side schools are not the same as the south side schools."

The public school into which her sons were placed did not meet her standards in a number of ways. Everyday classroom life was rowdy, and she became dismayed by her children's attempts to "fit in" by assimilating into what she characterized as the school's academically and socially dysfunctional culture. Teachers would spend most of the time in the classroom attempting to discipline children. "By the time they get the classroom under control, it's time to go home, and move to the next class."

According to Ms. Murphy, teachers who presided over such classrooms were not held accountable by school administrators. "You probably would have a hundred kids coming and telling you about one teacher. But, you know, they don't have the time to go and actually watch this particular teacher." To make matters worse, the school her sons attended compensated for its inability to achieve productive classroom environments by hiring cadres of security guards, who gave the school a quasi-militaristic feel. "[The school had] more security than the police department. And the police were constantly there, and whatever a student did, 'You're going home!' So they would do stuff so they could go home!" Ms. Murphy points out that such a disciplinary measure might have been momentarily helpful for a particular teacher, "But not for the kid. If they breathe hard, they're sending them home."

Ms. Murphy also found herself deeply incensed by the level of suspicion with which the public school regarded her children. When it was discovered that her son had gotten a ride with another student at the school—in a vehicle that the other child had taken on a test drive without returning—the school's principal blamed Ms. Murphy's son equally for the alleged crime. Although her son had assumed the vehicle belonged to the young man's mother, the principal "told my son, in front of me, 'What would make you do something like that? Next time you do something, you're out of here. You're going to alternative.'" Ms. Murphy realized that, in a school environment in which the principal was quick to treat students as criminals, such attitudes were likely to flow through the entire faculty. "If the head is speaking into that, then everybody ... you know, then ... he's passing it down, you know what I mean?"

Ms. Murphy faults "forced busing," and the closing of community schools, for many of these problems. Because schools are often distant from where families live, parents cannot keep tabs on the school and on their children. "You know, you [can't] walk down the street and check on your kid, especially if you're working downtown and the kid's going to school on up." Not only did forced busing impede parental involvement, but, according to Ms. Murphy, it also disadvantaged Black children relative to their White classmates. "All the Black kids were forced out of their neighborhoods. So you had to look at it, that you had to get up ... it was a hour ride to school, a hour ride home, that the White kids lived down the block and walked down the block home. So by the time we got home on the bus, they were already done with their homework."

Unlike the impersonality of the public schools that her children attended, where "they don't even know all of the kids in the school," Knowledge Ventures Learning Academy, according to Murphy, is the type of environment in which, "everybody ... knows me. Kids know me. I know all of the teachers. ... I could keep up with them better ... it was just a closer relationship." Although her children initially resisted the different culture of their new school, she feels that policies such as the requirement that students wear uniforms have helped her sons become more academically focused. "These children today ... are so hooked on fashion ... and the majority of the schools, especially the schools that are more Black populated ... the way those young girls dress at school, it's ridiculous how they allow it." Uniforms also pose less of a financial burden for Ms. Murphy, who no longer finds herself "trying to keep up with the expenses of trying to keep your kids with the peer pressure of the dress."

Not only does Ms. Murphy believe Knowledge Ventures is able to create relationships in which teachers and administrators "know what [students] are capable of doing, and if they're not doing what they should be doing," but it is also able to maintain productive classroom environments. "They have this school under ... it's really under control. It's like they don't have ... the rowdy mouths." According to Ms. Murphy, this is in part enabled by closer relationships with parents. Under such conditions antagonistic school–family relationships are less likely to develop, in which "you're trying to discipline a child, and then the parent want to come up and bless you out." With the help of parents, Knowledge Ventures' teachers and administrators are able to "stand on their rules more." Furthermore, she is aware that if teachers are not willing or able to cooperate with the school's disciplinary and academic objectives, the school is able to terminate their employment. "Each year I've noticed that if they don't evaluate well, they're gone." Due to a smaller environment, Ms. Murphy contends, the school's leaders "have a closer contact even with the teachers." Because administrators are more aware of problems among faculty, they respond more quickly in redirecting such teachers. Or, if necessary, they remove them from the school.

Although her sons initially "had a little smart little attitude and everything," her children eventually adjusted. In the few instances when her children still needed to be disciplined by the school, "instead of suspending them, they had like ... lunchroom duty. Or they had to clean the bathrooms." Ms. Murphy believes that this is "more of a discipline rather than sending them home, the parent's still at work."

Even though Ms. Murphy is generally deeply critical of public schools, she feels that the existence of the voucher program will help public schools to improve. "I believe it's going to bring a competition to the public schools. And which would force the public schools to address certain situations and deal with the children and, you know, focus more on the children instead of everything is financial." Furthermore, public schools would be aided "if they could just get some strong people."

Ms. Murphy also finds that many of the parents of public school students are partially accountable for the fact that, "the school system here stinks, bottom line." She explains, "you can't blame it all on the school system, because the parents, single parenting, single homes, single family homes have a lot to do with it. And parent involvement has a lot to do with it." Curiously, Ms. Murphy, who is of African descent, blames a dearth of parental involvement not just on forced busing, but also on supposedly Black cultural forms. "You know, this is a racial issue. Not racial, not just that … well I guess it is, due to race that, or different cultures, how they raise their children. And you know, and the Black race are very poor with keeping up with their children in school." Although she also denounces in strong language the negative effects of urban busing, and asserts that many parents are not able to adequately supervise their children's educational lives because they must work long hours, the distance that Ms. Murphy attempts to achieve in her choice of the pronoun "their" in describing what are supposedly the cultural attributes of Black people provides interesting insight into the subject positions that she is both trying to resist and inhabit. More will be said about this later.

Gary Johnson

As he openly explains, Gary Johnson is a former gang leader and ex-convict, and the father of two young women attending Knowledge Ventures Learning Academy.

> Now I'm not saying I'm a great parent or anything. I have my faults too. It's just that I've been through a lot, and I know what's out there. You know, I've always been a street person, until I started having kids. And then once I had [kids], it really made me change my life. Because I feel that most urban kids I would say—I wouldn't just say Black, because you have Hispanics, you have Chinese and Philippines and stuff like that—most people in the inner city only feel that they can do certain things. That's be dope dealers, pimps, prostitutes, thieves, or drug addicts. And you know, and there's more to life than that.

His primary objective with his daughters is to prevent them from making some of the wrong choices that he feels he made earlier in his life. And, according to Mr. Johnson, this is proving to be quite a challenge. "My youngest daughter has a behavior problem, and really the only person who can control her and contain her is me." He identifies a different sort of problem with his older daughter. "Her problem … was, she kind of like fell in love with this boy, so once he graduated, she really didn't want to go to school there."

Upon the advice of a cousin, Mr. Johnson moved his older daughter to Knowledge Ventures, where he had heard that children were eligible to work. "And so I'm like, okay, that's a foundation there." Although the promise of work turned out to be elusive, Mr. Johnson was amazed by the progress his daughter began making academically. "Right away her grades and everything just changed."

With his older daughter experiencing such success at the school, Mr. Johnson began wondering if enrolling his younger daughter there might prove beneficial as well. "My other daughter was constantly having ... problems, constantly having problems. So we got her in there." However, her difficulties were not ameliorated as swiftly as they were in the case of his older daughter. "Mind you, she had a problem when she got to [Knowledge Ventures]. Because she don't know how to keep her mouth quiet. She thinks she's a tough girl, and she's really not."

Immediately after the younger daughter's entrance into the school, "a conflict aroused itself, and the way they handled it made me feel real good." Because the school communicated the nature of the problem clearly to Mr. Johnson, he feels, the problem was resolved fairly quickly. "At first it was a misunderstanding, because I was hearing my daughter's version of it." He contrasts this with "what had really happened," as he soon learned from the school administration's version of events. Now he reports that his younger daughter enjoys school and gets good grades. He draws a sharp distinction between the disciplinary approach of Knowledge Ventures, in which, "they kind of like know how to deal with her, and how to work with her, because they took the time out," and the much less satisfactory disciplinary response of the public school his daughter previously attended. "Milwaukee Public Schools didn't take that initiative and try to get to know her."

Mr. Johnson also faults the Milwaukee Public Schools for their unwieldy size. "The classrooms are so big, they have so many students in them, there's no way that that teacher is going to get to know every student individually." At Knowledge Ventures, now that his older daughter is pregnant, he feels she receives the individualized attention and support that she needs within an educational context that Johnson refers to as "a good family." He further characterizes the school's climate as a balanced "chemistry," in which "it's a little playfullish, and it's a little bit like, I guess they can get hard-nosed. But I know, I've seen a lot of playfulness, and that's a good thing." His only complaint about the school's affective environment is "how some of the kids talk [to the teachers]." He attributes this perceived disrespect, for which his younger daughter was also disciplined, to "home training." "So I can't blame that on the teacher. The teacher just deals with it the best way they can."

Mr. Johnson also applauds the ability of the teachers at Knowledge Ventures to make the curriculum appealing, interesting, and relevant to students who have not always experienced schools as engaging places to be. "I believe that, like they say, the old saying goes, if you don't want a Black male to know anything, put it in a book, because they won't pick it up." At Knowledge Ventures, "they get creative, the teacher, to make them want to learn things." Particularly in relation to his daughter, "if she don't have any interest, I don't care how smart she is, she's not going to give you any of her knowledge, any of her input. And she's really interested in the school. ... They make my kids want to come to school. When I take my [church-related] trips out of town, they don't want to go. They want to go to school."

He feels the school has also succeeded in making connections with students' lives through the sense of trust administrators and teachers have earned from students in moments of school crisis. In one such incident, "I think a kid threatened to come back up to the school and shoot [it] up. ... They locked the whole parking lot down. And they were out there as a unit. I didn't see any police. I just saw the staff, and the security staff, where they could have called the police." Mr. Johnson elaborates:

> Because for someone to take the initiative like with that shooting situation, to go outside and don't have any police on the site. And they going to stand up there and act like police. They don't have the police, and that's a trust factor too. Because a lot of kids have little warrants that they haven't told the school about, and that brings the police. Now the police can check and screen people, so it's kind of like a trust factor.

This trust and respect is further instantiated in what Mr. Johnson sees as the school's commitment to families' cultural and religious preferences and requirements. He offers the following example: "[In the public schools] they feed all the kids the same thing. They don't have any—well, in high school they do—but in like elementary school they don't really have choices for a kid that don't eat pork. It's against their religion to eat pork." For Mr. Johnson, this creates a disharmonious school–home relationship in which, "it's hard to teach your child to be disciplined, and not to eat those things. You know, especially when they're young." According to Mr. Johnson, schools such as Knowledge Ventures are more likely to be responsive to such concerns because of their market-embedded relationship with their "customers."

Private schools, you tell them that, then, more than likely, you're paying them so they're going to really stick with it. ... Private schools [respect students and their families' wishes] because you're paying them. They have to do it. But public schools, they feel that, "Oh, this is a hopeless child. We're not going to ..." You know?

Although Mr. Johnson offers a consumerist model for understanding what he characterizes as the greater responsiveness of public schools, he also, paradoxically, faults public school teachers for being too narrowly focused on their own financial interests.

The majority of them is just there to get a paycheck ... That's not every teacher. ... You have some that really really want to help kids. And those are the ones that end up working at alternative schools, and end up going to private schools. Because they want to give back, you know. But the ones who don't really want to give back, they're just in it for the money ... majority of them work at the public schools. That's sad to say.

In the end, Mr. Johnson hopes that his own efforts, combined with those of the school, will lead his daughters toward a more satisfying young adult life than he experienced. He is confident that there are plenty of examples within his family that might help deter his daughters from replicating his earlier choices. "They have uncles that's incarcerated, and they want to be with them, but they can't be with them because they're incarcerated. There's things that they want to do with them, but they can't do. ... So they know that's not a place where they want to go. And plus, by me being an ex-con, they know how that felt by me not being at home, you know what I'm saying? They could come see me incarcerated. You know, that really didn't sit well with them."

Ramona Aguilar

Ramona Aguilar works at her church's food pantry, and is the foster mother of four children currently attending four different MPCP schools. Because Ms. Aguilar's English is relatively limited, our interview was interpreted by her oldest daughter (not one of the four attending MPCP schools), who currently works in the guidance counselor's office at Knowledge Ventures. "My mom has ... specifically has placed them in the Choice program, out of their schools, for the same exact reasons—one-on-one attention, and the dedication of the teachers, and the flexibility that they have towards the [parent–teacher] conferences and so on."

Ms. Aguilar's younger daughter transferred to Knowledge Ventures last year as a sophomore, after Ms. Aguilar became aware that her daughter, enrolled in a public high school, seemed to be "repeating a lot of her courses." As Ms. Aguilar's adult daughter explains:

> The courses in Milwaukee Public Schools, supposedly if you pass a course, then you move on to the next course if it's a second semester. However, if you look at her transcript, there are … it's the same course! Yes, at a different level, but only … it's just a extension that's different on the same course code. … So my sister was getting kind of bored and kind of antsy, because a person, when they get bored, they already know the stuff, what else can you do but, you know, start having some kind of disciplinary problems with that teacher because you've already learned it.

Ms. Aguilar feels that the "spiraling" curriculum practiced at the public school was not the only aspect that made this school less able to provide the kind of challenging and individually tailored education that she feels is of greatest benefit to her daughter. "The ratios are bigger, the class ratio to the teacher in public schools are much larger than at a small private or alternative." Under such overcrowded conditions, Ms. Aguilar wonders:

> How much time does it take a teacher to do roll call, limiting the instruction time? And then when you did have specific issues that you needed to talk to, the teacher does not have time in a public school. At [her previous public school] … she had 30 other students amongst her … So that was one of the reasons why [we] brought her here.

The overcrowded condition of her public school classroom, combined with the perceived repetitiveness of the curriculum, frustrated the daughter to the extent that the values Ms. Aguilar had taught her at home—to respect her teachers and other elders, for example—were being challenged and threatened.

Ms. Aguilar contrasts the attentiveness of teachers at Knowledge Ventures with the anonymity her daughter experienced at her public high school. She offers her experience with parent-teacher conferences as a case in point. At the public school's conferences, "They're all in the cafeteria, everything's set up in tables. You have two to three teachers per table.

... Teachers have to look for the 300 students that they see all day, and figure out, what they can just briefly tell [me] about [my] daughter." In contrast, at Knowledge Ventures, "you have that flexibility to go into the teacher's classroom, meet with that teacher, and everything that is said to the teacher, there's no one else to hear it." Furthermore, at her new school, "they're actually showing [me] everything that she had been doing in her classes. ... They've taken the time to give [me] a deep help parent–teacher conference." At conferences held in the cafeteria of the public school, "whatever they bring down is what they're showing [me]."

Ms. Aguilar blames what she regards as the poor conditions in public schools on two factors: inadequate funding—"things getting cut all the time"—and the fact that "teachers get such a high salary sometimes, that they ... it's the same if they teach, the same if they don't." She finds that this is particularly true of veteran teachers.

> Teachers that had been there 15 years or more were the ones that just didn't care, you know? It was worksheets, and no extreme teaching, no challenging. And so that classroom, you would go in there, you would have a lot of constant disciplinary problems. But yeah! You had disciplinary problems because the kids are bored and the teacher's fed up!

Ms. Aguilar attributes this teacher apathy not just to overcrowding, under-funding, and the disconnection between teachers' salaries and the success of their students. She also feels that such teachers are motivated by elitism. "Their class is higher than, you know, compared to the students' class."

While she is critical of many public school teachers, she also expresses sympathy for the way she feels they are overburdened. "They load you with so many things that, towards the end, you're tired. You don't feel like doing it no more because it's the overload. [You're] burnt out."

Johnson's Preparatory Academy

Johnson's Preparatory Academy is an independent nonsectarian MPCP school offering grades K4 through five in a remodeled two-story storefront building in northwest Milwaukee. The school's 66 students nearly all use vouchers to meet their tuition expenses. Ninety-two percent of the students enrolled are African American, and 8% are Latino/Latina. Sixty-four percent of the students are female. The school's six teachers provide "career-linked integrated thematic units of instruction" and partake in two-year collaborative teams.

Although Johnson's initially began as a low-income day care center, it has gradually expanded into the elementary grades. This year its first elementary cohort reached fifth grade, and the school's administration has decided to end the school's expansion at this threshold.

Reflecting its origins in day care provision, the school continues to provide early childhood training to W-2 participants (see endnote 2).

Farina Samuels

Farina Samuels is the mother of a fourth-grade boy who has attended Johnson's Preparatory Academy since the time that it expanded from a day care center to incorporate elementary school grades. Although Ms. Samuels is not familiar with the quality of education offered in most Milwaukee public schools, her impressions of her own public high school experiences in urban Chicago guided her in keeping her son in Johnson's once grade school became an option there. Although Ms. Samuels managed to keep her grades up as a child in Chicago's public schools—in part she believes because some of her teachers were of exceptional quality—nevertheless, she characterizes the general atmosphere of the schools as "wild."

Not only did Ms. Samuels want something different for her child, but she found herself frustrated by the very limited public school choices she encountered in Milwaukee. This differed markedly from the process of public school choice to which she had become accustomed growing up in Chicago.

The neighborhood public school in Milwaukee to which her son would likely have been assigned is actually closer to the Samuels' home than Johnson's Preparatory Academy. However, Ms. Samuels feared that her son would not fare well in an environment that she characterized as "sending a group of people to the class, and then trying to handle all of it." Within the anonymity and impersonality of such a schooling context, Ms. Samuels believes her child would easily be dismissed as "just being an 'out of order' child if he got in trouble."

She believes relationships with students are different at places like Johnson's, where "the teachers … get him going and kept his head straight." They accomplished this through "just concentration. It was just one-on-one. It wasn't a lot of the whole classroom thing. If something wasn't straight with that one—with him, then they would just deal with him." Rather than branding her child as a "problem child," "they kind of sat down and talked with him and us … and kind of worked it out."

The disadvantage of the relative distance of Johnson's Preparatory Academy from her home is mitigated by the free door-to-door transportation the school is able to offer. The perception of distance is further diminished by the "homey" atmosphere the school is able to cultivate, particularly because of its small size. "We know everybody here, especially since he's been there since it opened."

Furthermore, Ms. Samuels feels that the teachers at the school do a very good job keeping in touch with her about her son's progress. His tendency to become distracted has diminished considerably since the school began operating a system of rotating classrooms, on the model of a high school. "They are moving them around, so they get to meet all the teachers now. [They don't just] sit in the classroom all day, and then a lot of kids get distracted."

Ms. Samuels does not feel that private schools are inherently better than public schools. Instead, she indicates that she would put her child wherever she finds a quality learning environment. Now that her son is about to reach the final grade level offered at Johnson's, she is considering following the advice of the school's administrators—to enroll him, when the time comes, in a relatively successful public middle school in the area.

Tamara Robinson

Tamara Robinson's two older children attend fourth and fifth grade at Johnson's Preparatory Academy. Like Ms. Samuels, Ms. Robinson initially enrolled her children in Johnson's when it was exclusively a day care center. "And then they developed a school. And I was one of the parents who advocated for them to add grades." Her son, who is in fifth grade this year, will transfer at the end of the school year to a public middle school suggested by Johnson's principal. Ms. Robinson characterizes the public middle school as "a school for overachievers."

Again like Ms. Samuels, Ms. Robinson based her initial preference for a private school for her children on her impressions of public schools established when she was a child.

> The classrooms were so overwhelming with the amount of children in the classrooms that the teachers ... pretty much you were nobody until you made a name for yourself. You were either the smartest kid in the class, or the bully, or the class clown. And that's the only way that you got attention in the public school system.

She believes that her son would not have fared well in such an environment, given that "you wouldn't even know he was sitting there unless you actually looked at him. And he's very smart."

Ms. Robinson is enthusiastic about the way in which the curriculum at Johnson's Preparatory Academy is rooted in Howard Gardner's theory of "multiple intelligences."

> And that is really wonderful. I mean ... to have a child who likes music, and know how to work with their child, and not ... because the one that sticks out at my head the most, because we use it at our childcare center, is the child who's beating on things, and likes the music, likes the rhythm, and can get to the rhythm, and that's how he learns or she learns. And to the [public school] teacher, that's annoying. But it's actually what's making him into what he's going to be. It's helping cultivate who he is.

Whereas Ms. Robinson feels that such a teaching philosophy enables teachers to address the learning needs and preferences of a wide variety of students, her own memories of public school are that, "I haven't known any teacher to identify me as an individual. It was a conglomerate of kids ... You know, and I was supposed to be just like Sally, and Sally was just supposed to be like Johnny."

Ms. Robinson faults public schools for not cultivating a level of parental involvement that would maximize the benefit schools might bring to their students. Although Johnson's Preparatory Academy openly solicits its parents to become involved, Ms. Robinson has never been the type of parent who would be content to remain on the sidelines. Even though she works at two different day care centers, "I'm there probably about 3 days a week. Because both my day care centers ... the school's right in between. So when I'm going to one day care center I just stop in and see how everything is going. I'm probably a pest." Despite the fact that her children are only 10 and 11 years old, "I have picked the high schools and the junior high schools that my kids are going to go to since they were born. I know where they're going to go. I know that they're going to go to college."

In addition to soliciting and welcoming parental involvement, Ms. Robinson believes that Johnson's Preparatory Academy is also responsive to parents' concerns and suggestions. For Ms. Robinson, this is evident not only in the school's willingness to add on elementary grades. "They didn't have the computer lab in the beginning, but they got one. And a lot of the things that the parents voice their opinions about what they should have, they put in place. ... It's not where your opinions or your thoughts and ideas don't matter."

Johnson's also responded to families' requests that after-school activities be created so that children could remain supervised until their parents finished work. Now that after-school programs have been established, coupled with the school's commitment to deliver children directly to the doors of their homes at the end of the day, Ms. Robinson feels that her children are always in good hands. Although Milwaukee Public Schools also operates transportation services that accommodate her neighborhood, the nearest designated bus stop is five or six blocks away. Although this may not seem like a large distance, Ms. Robinson lives in a neighborhood of government-subsidized housing that has experienced considerable crime. "I almost just want to get into tears when I think about my kids being on a bus stop five blocks from me, and they're only 10 and 11 years old ... What happens between five and six blocks?"

Ms. Robinson contends that her biggest educational struggle is not with an unresponsive school, but rather with her husband of six years from whom she is now separated. According to Ms. Robinson, he shares neither her enthusiasm for private schools like Johnson's, nor her commitment to parental involvement. She anticipates that these tensions will come to a head as her youngest daughter, now 3 years old, approaches school age.

> Now my baby, I even have a bigger fight, because her father ... he doesn't want her to go to a Choice school. He wants her, he's strong on the public school. So she goes to a Head Start program right now, which is in the public sector, and we're trying it out. But I really want her to go to [Johnson's] for her first grade.

She contrasts her tendency to assess school quality through lengthy investigation and participation, with what she sees as his more superficial evaluation of potential schools. His disposition is, "Well, what's wrong with the public schools? They've been up all these years." She continues:

> To him, what looks good on the outside is good. That's what everybody in the public school system sees, is it looks like a nice bright school, the floors are clean, the walls are clean—you know, this must be the way to

go. It doesn't matter what the product is when it's done. It's just that it looks clean, it looks good, they have qualified teachers.

She feels that such superficial assessments can spell trouble for parents at both public and private schools. "Because, you know, you've got a lot of Choice programs giving out computers. And you know, a lot of different schools doing different things to get children in. But I don't know what they do as far as their program goes."

Ms. Robinson also contrasts the compassion she feels from teachers at Johnson's to the antagonism that she believes pervades parent–teacher relationships in public schools. "It's not where, 'Your kid is this! And your kid is that.'" When Ms. Robinson initially considered a public school near their house six years ago, on her first visit to the school she was frightened by the interactions she witnessed between teachers and students. In one instance,

> I went and I interviewed the school, and I filled out an application, and a teacher was dragging [a student] down the hallway ... and the child was fighting a little bit, you know kind of wrestling. And she's like, "You're going to sit your butt right there, and you're not going to move!" ... It's just, "I can't put up with him anymore!" And threw him in the chair and walked off ... And that was enough for me.

To Ms. Robinson, such behavior approaches the level of child abuse, particularly given that "a teacher is like ... to a little kid is almost like a god ... I mean they hold them up so high."

Although the middle school her son will soon enter is a public school, Ms. Robinson is fairly confident, based on the school's reputation, that the quality of relationships at the school will differ significantly from those she witnessed at the public school she visited previously. Still, she does have some concerns. "My son is not going to be used to that. It's a big school." Some of her friends have cautioned her that even at this public middle school, which largely caters to students labeled talented and gifted, "the kids are mean, the kids are rude ... it's just like another junior high school." Furthermore, Ms. Robinson, who is European-American, invokes the following racialized characterization of her chosen middle school and Milwaukee public schools in general: "Even though it's a gifted and talented school, it doesn't mean that, you know ... There's still neighborhood kids that go there. So Milwaukee public schools is like that. Just because it's gifted and talented, about 30% of the neighborhood kids is going there."

Despite the fact that she anticipates some trouble for her son at the public middle school, she also feels her son "might actually fit in a little bit better" there. "It wasn't easy for him though, even at [Johnson's], because he's a biracial child. And that school's primarily Black kids. So it wasn't … he did feel some ridicule, and he felt different even there. So it wasn't like he's not familiar with what he'll go through."

Although she believes that parents need to carefully investigate the schools they choose for their children, she recognizes that "not all parents have the time to do that." Despite this, she feels that the existence of the voucher program will compel Milwaukee Public Schools to improve. It was this that she kept in the back of her mind "when we were going to go to Madison and fight for the Choice program."

> My whole thought was that Milwaukee Public Schools had a lot to worry about, and Choice programs really don't, because when you look at the program, and you look at the differences, Milwaukee Public Schools should be worried. They should really reevaluate their program. And if you want to get kids, it shouldn't … I guess what I'm trying to say is like Ameritech. You shouldn't be able to monopolize the whole thing. There should be a choice. … And that can only bring up their standards. You know, Milwaukee Public Schools has to raise up their standards.

When asked if she had noticed evidence that Milwaukee Public Schools was moving in the direction she indicated, she responded, "I haven't seen any demonstrations of that at all." Instead, as a day care worker, she has "seen them hit another sector, which hurt the day care center." Alluding to Milwaukee Public Schools' creation of before- and after-school day care centers, she continues:

> I have not seen them enrich their programs. I've seen them just change their direction to where they're going. And Milwaukee Public Schools is really cutthroat. You know, I mean, in the beginning, when the wraparound program started, I didn't see why they were doing it. My whole thing is, stick to what you're doing, and, you know, make that better. Why would you want to open up a day care center and you don't have your other program right? But the parents, a lot of parents don't think of it like that. There's a lot who will say, "Oh wow! They have a day care center after school, or a day care center before school." But their *school* program is not good.

According to Ms. Robinson, in the final analysis, Milwaukee Public Schools have indeed responded to market pressures brought about by the creation of the MPCP—but not in ways that she feels are beneficial or educationally desirable. Although "cutthroat" maneuvers within an educational market are supposed to lead to increased efficiency and responsiveness to parents, instead they have led to duplication of services, the erosion of the private sector industry in which Ms. Robinson is involved, and the drifting of Milwaukee Public Schools away from what she feels should be its core focus—providing grade school education for Milwaukee's children.

Silvia Danford

All three of Silvia Danford's sons have attended Johnson's Preparatory Academy for several years. Her two younger sons, currently in second and fourth grade, have attended Johnson's since they became school age and her oldest son, now in fifth grade, started school in the Milwaukee Public Schools.

Ms. Danford also has two older daughters who have never attended private school, and are currently enrolled in a public middle school. "And it seems like the boys ... they are basically on the same level as my daughters."

But Ms. Danford's negative impressions of Milwaukee public schools are not just rooted in her daughters' poor achievement.

> I went to public school. It was 33 or 34 children in a classroom, and if you did not really know what you're doing, and the teacher ... you were lost ... you'd just be lost, because the teacher couldn't give you individual attention. Like with each child, she couldn't spend 20 minutes on each child.

When her oldest son initially entered public school, he experienced many of the same classroom conditions that she had endured as a child. When he began to have problems with reading, she knew she would need to look elsewhere to address her son's situation. Although she knows his public school teacher was very well intended and skilled, Ms. Danford realized the teacher was hamstrung by overwhelming classroom conditions.

> I feel sorry for her. She had 34 students. And she had someone come in. But those two teachers—I mean think about it. Thirty-three people between two people. That's a lot. And it was hard. She made flash cards, and [was] telling me how to work with them. But she really couldn't

put the on-hand that she wanted to do. And I know that she was stuck, because that's the way, you know, that's her job.

Although the teacher remained stuck in conditions that she neither chose nor felt she could change, Ms. Danford felt she could alleviate her oldest son's predicament by way of the voucher program. She contrasts the public school conditions that she, her two daughters, and older son experienced with the classroom environments her son began to experience at Johnson's.

> I know with the smaller classroom it's easier to address the problem quicker. You notice it, you know, more faster than you would if you have more kids. ... The classes are smaller, so that gives teachers more time to work with children individually, and to help them more. The class size is very important to me, because I know the child could have more hand-on-hand, teaching with the teacher, or the specialist in the classroom ... could work with them individually on [their] activities.

Ms. Danford believes her oldest son's new school has brought great improvement. "His reading is picking up since he's been to this school for sure. Because they spend so much time on each subject." Furthermore, students are much more challenged with homework. "They got it every night. My [youngest] son ... he's seven. He's had homework every night, and that's good. He has more homework than my daughters in middle school."

In addition to smaller class sizes, Ms. Danford also appreciates the intimacy that a small school environment such as Johnson's is able to achieve. "It seems like it's more of a home environment. It's like partly day care and school together. It's like ... they're growing together. They become like a second family."

Furthermore, the school as a whole offers an approach to curriculum and pedagogy with which Ms. Danford is highly satisfied. "It's like ... Montessori ... like hands on. So it's like, get to the solution, but use your own methods for getting there. But with Milwaukee Public Schools ... they have to do it exactly the way teachers teach them ... That can be difficult to a child too. Hurt a child too."

She appreciates other aspects of the curriculum as well, particularly as they have benefited her oldest son in overcoming his reading difficulties. "Their reading readiness program was excellent. They get a sheet with master words that they can use to sound out other words and learn vocabulary words." And, "I think the math too. All my children are advanced in math, because they teach them different formulas how to get to the answer."

In fact, Ms. Danford feels that she would have benefited greatly as a college student had she been exposed to such methods in grade school. Upon entering college, "We had to retrain our thinking and our learning and everything else. I wound up studying ... we didn't know how to write things that were on our own. So we had to go back and relearn everything basically from the other students."

She contrasts the "innovative" methods of Johnson's with her daughters' experiences at public middle school. Her daughters rarely seem to have homework, and they do not have textbooks they can bring home.

> She says she has a handbook ... I know some schools, they use handbooks where the teacher makes copies. I don't like that method too much, because I can't see what they're doing; can't see where to help them. So if they could make a change, and get more current books. Or get all the children workbooks that they could take home.

Because of the improvements she perceives the availability of vouchers has brought to the educational lives of her children, Danford hopes that the program continues. "I think the parents deserve the option of deciding public or Choice. Because, you know, we're all taxpayers here. So we're paying. I work here [at Boston Store] every day. So absolutely. Though ... I have a choice in the matter too, because I'm a voter too."

Marcus Garvey Academy

Marcus Garvey Academy, the final school in this study, promotes itself as a school committed to "African-centered" curricula and pedagogy. According to the school's literature, its mission is deeply rooted in Black nationalist philosophies. The school professes particular allegiance to calls by Black economic nationalists for the creation of all-Black political, economic, social, and cultural institutions. Such independent institutions, according to the school's principal, would end dependence on White-controlled institutions that, although often claiming otherwise, actually perpetuate poverty among Blacks. Marcus Garvey Academy, with its interior walls adorned by artwork based on Nile River and Pan-Africanist themes, is offered as an antidote to this tendency.

Housed in a drab former church building, Marcus Garvey enrolls 84 students in grades K4 through eight. All of the school's students are African American, and all students use a voucher in order to meet tuition expenses.

Shirley Munson

Shirley Munson's son, Charles, attends the fifth grade at Marcus Garvey Academy. Although her son was initially enrolled in a public charter school, his kindergarten teacher suggested that Munson transfer him to a private school, because Charles, according to the teacher, was "very smart, but … he moves around." Ms. Munson followed the teacher's advice, transferring her son for first grade into a private Lutheran school with an excellent reputation. But at the Lutheran school, the teacher "had 26 kids in the classroom, no aide, and she had 7 or 8 boys like [Charles]. So [Charles] stayed in the hall." By second grade "the breakdown came. It was eight kids like [Charles] in the hallway … Well, I didn't send [Charles] to school to be in the hallway."

Ms. Munson points out that her son's classmates at the Lutheran school were overwhelmingly White. "Now he wasn't the only Black child, but he was the darkest child. … I think that had a lot to do with her not knowing how to do with him."

Ms. Munson is convinced that her son lost considerable ground both academically and socially that year. "He wouldn't make eye contact with [the teacher] … He might have lost a year just being traumatized, sitting out in the hallway, not being able to make eye contact, kids not liking him, not hardly inviting him to their little birthday parties. So he was just really outcast." When the school advised that he be held back a year because he seemed immature, "I said I had to take him out of there before they kill him, before they destroy him."

Not knowing quite what to do, Ms. Munson had her son tested through Milwaukee Public Schools. "[They] said he could go to school. There was no need to hold him back, because academically he was on task." One day while driving, Ms. Munson spotted the sign for Marcus Garvey Academy on the side of the old church building. "And I had a friend that just happened to work here. And [the principal] was kind enough to let [Charles] come. He was in the second grade. I pulled him right out."

Ms. Munson is not just being polite when she refers to the principal's generosity in accepting her child. "He took him in March. There was no financial benefit for him. Because anybody you take, you know, after a certain time [isn't counted in the school's enrollment]. So he took him just because that's the kind of man he is."

Although Ms. Munson knows that her son's experiences at the Lutheran school were harmful, she still retains some sympathy for the personnel of the school.

> I felt bad for that woman ... They wanted [Charles] to continue. So they just didn't understand ... And they have an excellent program. It just almost destroyed [Charles] though. Not intentionally, I don't believe it was, but ... I think it was just too much of a burden on her. She had 26 kids, she had no aide. She would come fresh in the morning, eyes blood-shot in the evening. You know, it was terrible for her. And so to have like eight boys. ... And then they wanted to M-Team him, they wanted to test him, and ... there's nothing wrong with him, you know, other than he has just a little bit more energy. So I wasn't going through that. And so here, it's not required. He excels in his academics. There was no need for me to have him M-Teamed simply because he's not as still as they wanted him to be. And that was important. They wanted him still because they've got 26 or more kids in the room.

At Marcus Garvey Academy, Ms. Munson's son was no longer viewed through a lens of pathology. "They understood how to work with [Charles] and all his moving around. He started making eye contact, whereas when you used to speak with him he would look down. His self-esteem just really shot up."

Now, three years later, Ms. Munson works in the school's office as an administrative assistant, and several of her grandchildren attend the school. "Two of them are in kindergarten, and one of them is in the first grade. They're reading, they're writing, because our K4, K5 program is accelerated." At Marcus Garvey, "the classrooms are smaller, and we do have aides." Because of the high adult to student ratio, Ms. Munson explains, children who want to move around are not regarded as much of a problem. When more serious problems arise, the school rarely needs to rely on suspensions. Because there is good contact with parents, Ms. Munson has found that "we nip it in the bud, right away."

Although she is very satisfied with her son's circumstances at Marcus Garvey, she does not feel that private schools are necessarily better than public schools. She regards her original decision to pull Charles from a public charter school and place him in the private Lutheran school as a mistake. In fact, there is a public school in her neighborhood to which she would consider sending her children today. "Right up the street from me, there's a school where people come from some of the ... from suburbs." Unfortunately for Ms. Munson and her children, the school is a magnet school. "It's public, but private. My kids couldn't go, and it's right up the street." In addition to the magnet school, another school nearby is a public Montessori school. "Those are the two schools that I would have chosen, but I wasn't able to," due to selective admissions policies. "You know, so then my babies would have went. But otherwise ... I had a choice of [the regular public school]. Nobody wants their kids at [that school]. That's a public school. In Milwaukee. Nobody wants their kids there. That's a dumping ground."

Patrice King

Patrice King is the mother of three children, two of whom presently attend Marcus Garvey Academy. She did not consider transferring her older son, currently enrolled in a public elementary school, into Garvey because she was concerned about the potential negative effects of discontinuity in his school experiences.

Her middle son, in first grade at Marcus Garvey, initially enrolled in another MPCP school. But Ms. King became dissatisfied with the school after sensing that relationships among staff and students were for the most part not ones built upon mutual respect. Ms. King speculates that for this reason, teachers were not very successful with their students. Given the school's relatively inhospitable climate, she also resented that parental involvement was mandatory.

Although parental involvement at Marcus Garvey Academy is not mandatory, Ms. King is extremely active in the school and assists in classrooms regularly. Due to her active involvement, she has been able to observe first-hand the kinds of positive relationships she believes the school cultivates. Ms. King has also learned a considerable amount about the school's curriculum, with which she is very pleased. She finds the school's African-centeredness to be an asset in helping her sons build self-confidence. Her child in first grade is doing so well that he will advance to the third grade in the year to come. Most of all, she values Marcus Garvey Academy's small-school atmosphere and small class sizes.

Based on her own experiences as well as those of her children, Ms. King has concluded that desirable and undesirable schools exist in both public and private education. Although she is content with the public school her fifth grader currently attends, she remembers her own public school experiences as significantly less positive. Ms. King attended public schools in Milwaukee through high school, and recalls that beginning at the middle school level, classroom environments were almost invariably chaotic. Now as her oldest son goes about the process of selecting a middle school, she plans to make certain that he does not end up in a similar environment.

Ms. King characterizes public school classrooms in general as overcrowded. Such large class sizes, she feels, deprive students of individual attention and quality relationships with their teachers. Rather than blaming public school teachers for these characteristics, though, Ms. King expresses sympathy for the overwhelming and overcrowded conditions in which many teachers must struggle to educate children.

Ella Mosley

Ella Mosley is a teacher's aide in her first year at Marcus Garvey Academy. She has five children enrolled in the school at a variety of grade levels. She regards two of her children, twin daughters in fifth and sixth grade, as "very slow." One of her twins has had such acute learning difficulties that she was held back a grade. Ms. Mosley also has two older daughters who transferred to Marcus Garvey from a public middle school, who she laments are also now "very far behind."

Ms. Mosley chose Garvey only after

> They tried a public school first. And that was not working out as far as they academics and things like that. I needed a slower pace for them, a smaller classroom environment ... because sometime the teacher don't have time for them to, you know, to give them that one on one time. Or break it down to them, where they need to learn it at.

In addition to the lack of accommodation for her daughters' educational needs, she feels the disciplinary policies in the public middle school were not oriented to the family's best interests. "I was constantly having to be out at the school trying to see what's going on ... The environment they were around made them stay in the hallways, made them slowly be kicked out ... It wasn't a thing where they sat in the classroom and got that one on one." At Marcus Garvey Academy, "They can't run around and nobody can influence them ... on going out of the class or whatever. They got that one on one where the teacher is focused on them."

Ms. Mosley feels that such a focus is particularly important for her daughters experiencing difficulties with the pace of their education, "because once they start falling behind, they don't want to … school don't interest them no more."

Not only does Garvey provide a greater focus on the academic development of her daughters, but with the help of the school she is also able to keep better tabs on their behavior. "They let me know right away." This contrasts sharply with experiences her children have had at both public schools and at another voucher school two of them previously attended. At the public school, teachers "waited until the situation gets worser and then they call you once they get suspended. And it's like, 'Hey, your child is suspended, too!' So, you know, why did the problem get worse to the point where I didn't get a call before now to let me know what my child is doing?" Similarly, at the voucher school her daughters previously attended, "instead of the teacher just dealing with the situation … they wouldn't even call. They would just say, 'Well, you know, your child is suspended for such and such.' They wait until the problem gets worser instead of calling and letting you know." Such disciplinary practices are not only neglectful of the best interests of her children, but they also present a significant financial burden for her family. "Then they got to be at home for three days. Then that slows me up for them being out for three days because I wasn't aware what they were doing before now." At Garvey, not only is there better contact between the school and its subscribing families, but "since she's been here … she can't roam the halls. It's small."

Ms. Mosley concludes, "A lot of people probably wouldn't agree with Choice schools, but they really work for some parents that have problem kids, or that have children that they can't control. I mean … the schools like this can help them to bring them out better, as far as going out there and messing theyself up in the outside."

In the next chapter, I utilize the data organized and only preliminarily analyzed here in order to assess the nature of the articulations that take place between the various levels of the African American component of the voucher alliance and more powerful conservative groups and tendencies. I also examine the nature of the agency that is present in the articulations that these parents and guardians have formed with the voucher movement.

6

FROM MAKING DO TO REMAKING ALLIANCES: A CALL FOR PROGRESSIVE MODERNIZATION IN EDUCATION AND BEYOND

When I formed a coalition with Tim Sheehy [Director of the Metropolitan Milwaukee Association of Commerce] and the Catholic Archdiocese and all those people who say they support us, I did so because it was a way of helping my parents. I knew all along they didn't care about my children. They cared about their agenda. ... Powerful interests such as the MMAC have no moral authority in our community. If they really cared about our community the way they say, we would not be in such dire need right now. They have all the power and money in their hands. They could help make the conditions better in our community. But they don't.

Wisconsin State Representative Polly Williams,
quoted in Miner, 1997

To what extent do the discourses of African American families utilizing vouchers coincide with the discourses of conservative modernization? Clearly there is some overlap, as illustrated, for example, by repeated dissatisfaction with some actions taken by teachers unions. Yet significant divergence from neoliberal and neoconservative discourses (e.g., concerning faith in educational markets and the supposed pathology of the urban poor) signals that the bond between African American voucher families and their more powerful partners in the voucher alliance may not be as cemented as it initially appears. Are there other educational visions that would more effectively address voucher families' educational concerns?

The answer to this question can best be approached through an inventory, drawn from the narratives of the MPCP families in the preceding chapter, of the ways in which vouchers represent at least a partial solution to many African American families.

All three Mariama Abdullah school parents—Alexis Turner, Sonia Israel, and Darla Kelly—mentioned the importance of small class sizes. According to the three women, smaller classes enable teachers to be more in touch with the real life circumstances of students and their families. A reduced student load furthermore allows teachers to provide individual attention and differentiated instruction. Discipline becomes more manageable, as teachers cope more effectively because of a closer relationship with both student and family. The ability to respond faster to problems that arise, because of a smaller number of overall students presenting difficulties, allows teachers to prevent small issues from becoming larger ones. Small class size, according to Darla Kelly, even fosters accountability, as teachers become less able to claim that they're too overwhelmed to stay in touch with parents. As a result of closer and therefore more transparent relationships, teachers with smaller classes are less empowered to allege student pathology as a cover for their own inadequacies.

Besides attributing great importance to small class size, the Mariama Abdullah parents all stressed the importance of a smaller, more tightly knit school. Such schools have more of a family feeling, they said, which helps to keep the more negative directions that students' lives might take in check. There is also more potential for staff unity.

In one way or another, all three parents emphasized that the right morals and values are needed to guide the school. Although Kelly did not believe it was the role of the school to sow morals into supposedly amoral students, she did want to protect her child from morally loose and wild teachers who she felt might try to get her child involved in things of which she did not approve. Although Turner is not a Muslim, she too appreciates the ethical and moral focus of the school, including its connectedness to the surrounding community. Israel also contrasts the values orientation of the Mariama Abdullah School to the moral vacuum she had encountered in public schools.

Although the three parents found these desirable elements in their chosen school, they characterized schools they had rejected—both public and private—in the following manner. Israel and Kelly both spoke about the racial stigmatization their families had encountered in schools in which their children were previously enrolled. Turner likewise narrated her experience of helping her niece to escape the raced and pathological frames that were being attached to her. In the same vein, Turner spoke about the importance of teachers understanding students as situated beings, rather than misreading them through a normative middle-class lens.

All three parents expressed sympathy for teachers who struggled in overcrowded conditions. Such teachers were not adequately assisted by administrators, were not able to provide the differentiated instruction and individual attention that would best serve their students, and struggled to cope with too many challenging children concentrated into one classroom. Furthermore, teachers were underpaid and, understandably, prone to "burning out."

Although all three expressed sympathy for teachers, two of the three—Israel and Kelly—had harsh words for teachers unions, which they blamed for protecting incompetent teachers and for largely serving their own narrow interests. Israel identified not only the teachers unions, but also the sheer size of the public school system as obstacles that kept teachers and administrators from finding common purpose in serving the educational interests of the schools' children.

In regard to education within a market context, Israel stressed the need for the state to regulate participating schools as a mechanism for assuring parents that schools were offering proper facilities, licensed teachers, effective instruction, and adequate learning materials. Otherwise, schools might be patched together for the sole purpose of profiting unsavory opportunists. Whereas Israel emphasized regulation, Turner depicted struggling families who would find great difficulty in acting as empowered consumers within an educational marketplace. Such families would also have a difficult time meeting a school's expectations concerning parental involvement. Despite these explicit and implied reservations about educational markets, both Israel and Kelly tactically adopted the conservative market-grounded identity of "taxpayer" as a way of countering the poor school conditions and pejorative subject positions that their families were offered.

If Turner, Israel, and Kelly were to delineate their ideal agenda for schools, it could safely be presumed to include the following: the school would have small class sizes, a faculty united by a common vision, a values-oriented curriculum rooted in students' lives and the community within which the school was embedded. Rather than pathologizing students and their families, schools would understand them as situated beings frequently struggling with significant challenges in their personal lives. Furthermore, such schools would be regulated to ensure that school facilities were up to standards and that teachers were properly licensed. Responsibility for "regulating" the school could not simply be devolved to parents, who are often too overwhelmed with other responsibilities to leverage schools into proper behavior. Finally, unions would need to broaden their focus beyond teachers' narrow self-interests, and would have to stop protecting and start disciplining ineffective, racist, and destructive teachers.

Before assessing the educational visions of the families associated with the other four schools in this study, I want to pose the following questions. Is this a conservative agenda? Are there elements of neoliberal and neoconservative educational visions in this agenda, and can it be articulated to a conservative agenda? Have parents been able to get some of the things they desired educationally from such an articulation? Could such an agenda be articulated to progressive movements within education? Would such a progressive educational agenda, if actionable, more effectively meet parents' educational needs and interests? Do progressives have the resources—materially, politically, and culturally—to actualize such an agenda? What is better in the long run for urban working-class and poor families of color—disarticulating their agenda from that of conservatives, or leaving the articulation intact?

As with the parents of Mariama Abdullah School, each of the parents of St. Urbina—Dasha Dapedako, Gina Price, and Jan Lincoln—emphasize the deleterious effects of overcrowding in schools. Big classes and big schools lead to conditions in which the management of misbehaving students takes precedence over academic and social curriculum, school officials are not sufficiently communicative with parents, and teachers are not able to provide the individual attention and differentiated instruction that children need. At a school like St. Urbina, which can offer a small school environment and small class sizes, the parents assert that academics are regarded with the seriousness to which students are entitled. Behavioral problems are quickly managed, in part because of stronger relationships teachers are able to forge with parents and students, and teachers are able to provide more individualized attention and the kind of differentiated curriculum that enables a wide variety of students to do well. Disciplinary policies are rooted in forms that recognize the socioeconomic class-based situatedness of the school's families.

Because St. Urbina is an all-girls school that requires uniforms, all three parents felt that the twin distractions of competition over fashion and boys were avoided. As a result, the young women of the school became more absorbed in their studies, and benefited from the positive attribution given by the school to its significant racial, ethnic, cultural, socioeconomic, and linguistic diversity. Furthermore, parents note that St. Urbina has high expectations and offers a challenging curriculum to all students regardless of their background. The school, according to the parents, believes that students can do well, and wants them to do well. Although the school is challenging, it does not privilege investigative forms of learning that exclude previously underserved students by assuming that they have already attained "the basics." Curriculum is not centralized, enabling teachers to tailor a de-centered school curriculum to their students' particular needs and interests.

Of the three parents from St. Urbina, only one—Ms. Dapedako— explicitly located herself ideologically within the multiple discourses intersecting the MPCP. For her, vouchers are to be supported because they are a form of state-sponsored redistributive justice, which gives parents like her access to some of the same opportunities privileged families already enjoy. These are the same families who should be footing the bill for the program. Dapedako believes her children have a right to quality education because, like many other parents of her income stratum, she has worked hard to provide for her family. Vouchers are a means through which the state lives up to its obligations within a social contract; and through which marginalized families are able to obtain choice—defined as the ability of all families to send their kids to schools of the caliber of St. Urbina.

Furthermore, according to Dapedako, teachers are undervalued, underpaid, and prone to burnout. Along with teachers, schools, if they are to adequately serve low-income urban populations, need the same money and the same access to resources that other, more privileged schools already enjoy.

Unlike Dapedako, Price and Lincoln do not explicitly situate themselves ideologically. Nevertheless, their conviction that public schools are primarily impeded by overcrowded classrooms differs sharply from neo-liberal positions, which hold that poorly performing urban public schools are the result of inefficiencies created by self-protective teachers unions and the monopolistic "producer capture" of urban education by bloated self-serving bureaucracies.

Furthermore, in their calls for differentiated instruction, situated forms of discipline, and relevant, flexible curriculum, the St. Urbina parents express support for forms of curriculum and pedagogy that run counter to neoconservative calls for a standardized and universal "common curriculum."

Again, from the content of the three interviews with parents and guardians at Knowledge Ventures—Samantha Murphy, Gary Johnson, and Ramona Aguilar—we can discern some of the concerns and ideas about education that drive families away from Milwaukee public schools and toward the voucher-accepting school of their choice. All three Knowledge Ventures parents and guardians emphasize the importance of a supportive, family-type school environment. Each contrasts this to the anonymity, impersonality, and even elitism that they perceive in most public school environments.

This relatively more intimate school atmosphere leads to closer communication between the school and its subscribing families. Closer relationships also allow for more appropriate forms of discipline, which the school attempts to situate within the realities of students' and parents' everyday lives.

Unlike public school classrooms, which all three characterized as unruly and overcrowded, Knowledge Ventures' classrooms are seen as more academically focused and productive. Teachers can offer one-on-one attention tailored to students' individual needs. Additionally, because the school's curriculum is more decentralized than that of Milwaukee Public Schools, it is more easily adapted to students' interests, needs, and preferred learning modalities.

Not only do public schools suffer from large class and school sizes, they are also impeded by unequal and inadequate funding and the lack of administrative flexibility in redirecting or terminating less successful teachers. According to Samantha Murphy, schools compensated for an inability to control overcrowded classroom environments by hiring security guards, thereby giving the schools an alienating militaristic feel. At such schools, discipline is frequently not appropriate to students' home contexts, and ends up harming students more than it helps them.

The Knowledge Ventures' parents also noted that public schools (and many of their students) must contend with the negative consequences of "forced busing"—reduced parental involvement and travel-weary students. Because of the lack of enforceable school uniform policies, the parents asserted, public schools are beset by a fashion show environment that is distracting to students and costly to parents and guardians.

According to Johnson and Murphy, public schools are not as responsive to families' concerns as they might be because their personnel do not perceive themselves to be involved in a market relationship with their parent-customers. At the same time, teachers are too narrowly interested in their own financial well-being and are paid whether or not they are successful with children. In contrast to this, teachers at Knowledge Ventures are perceived to be more motivated by their dedication to their students.

Because public schools are frequently beset with irrelevant or unchallenging curricula, as well as unruly classrooms, they are seen by Aguilar as a threat to traditional home values such as respect for one's elders. However, all three parents expressed some degree of sympathy with teachers' working conditions, and Johnson and Murphy blame the problems public schools experience at least partially on "poor home training" and the supposed pathology of Black cultural forms.

What is again perhaps most interesting in the comments and concerns expressed by the Knowledge Ventures' parents and guardians is the way in which they mobilize discourses in hybrid fashion. The manner in which this is done makes it very difficult to locate them within a particular discursive or ideological "camp," either within debates around educational marketization or within debates around the broader direction of the U.S. social formation and state.

As mentioned, we see Johnson and Murphy invoking primarily neoconservative themes in faulting "home training" and the supposed pathology of Black cultural forms. Furthermore all three Knowledge Ventures families touched upon themes that would best be described as neoliberal—that administrators should have more flexibility in hiring, firing, and disciplining their teachers; that competition brought by the voucher program will also benefit students in the public schools, as Milwaukee Public Schools is forced to become competitive; and that schools will become responsive to their subscribing families to the degree that they are made to realize that they are embedded in a market relationship with their parent-customers.

However, we also find currents within interviews that run counter to neoliberal and neoconservative thinking around education. For example, each of the parents and guardians at Knowledge Ventures, like the parents and guardians at the other schools discussed so far, stressed above all the importance of small class size. Not only do many neoliberals and neoconservatives take issue with the emphasis that educational progressives place on small class size in urban educational reform, but they furthermore contend that if small class sizes were really what urban educational customers wanted, educational markets would deliver them. What prevents public schools from having small class sizes is neither their unresponsiveness to parents, nor their lack of efficiency. Clearly, the Knowledge Ventures' parents asserted, public school teachers would want smaller class sizes, and Milwaukee Public Schools is aware of the importance of small class sizes to the families of central Milwaukee. What prevents public schools from having small class sizes is the funding that would enable this.

The very same parent who highlighted the supposedly deleterious effects of Black cultural forms—Samantha Murphy—also denounced her son's public school principal for failing to see her child outside of a deeply raced frame of criminality and suspicion.

Clearly parental articulations to the educational and social visions of conservative modernization are not something that conservatives have simply "won." Rather these articulations are still very much in formation. The hybridity of parents' discourses concerning the dysfunctionality of many urban public schools leaves considerable space for their rearticulation to ultimately more effective and democratic educational reform movements.

The themes that the parents of Johnson's Preparatory Academy raise in their narratives about navigating educational options within the City of Milwaukee, although occasionally unique, also resonate with those of parents and guardians of children enrolled in the previous MPCP schools discussed. Public school teachers are characterized by Farina Samuels, Tamara Robinson, and Silvia Danford as overwhelmed by the rebellious behavior of their students and unable to provide the individualized one-on-one attention and differentiated, hands-on curriculum that they believe their students need.

The relatively large size of most public schools leads to insufficiently communicative relationships with parents that are frequently fraught with antagonism. Through the eyes of these parents, parental involvement is not effectively solicited by most public schools, and is often not even welcome.

Parents' primary communication with the school occurs only after their children have managed to attract attention to themselves through misbehavior or poor academic achievement. Even then, interactions between teachers and parents are often volatile exchanges in which families learn that their child has been dispatched with the racialized classification of "problem child."

In contrast, because of Johnson's Preparatory Academy's small class sizes and small school size, children who do not meet expectations, according to the parents I interviewed, are approached constructively as situated beings. Teachers are able to stay in regular contact with parents and understand the complex situations children and their families face. Parental involvement is welcomed and encouraged, and the school is responsive to the requests and concerns that families raise. A "safe" school environment is further extended through after-school activities that run into the late afternoon, and children are delivered door to door by the school's free transportation system.

Within Johnson's classrooms, parents felt that students were challenged by an engaging hands-on curriculum that encouraged divergent thinking and which they were able to access through a range of learning modalities.

Despite their level of contentment with Johnson's Preparatory Academy, all three parents expressed that private schools are not inherently superior to public schools. Samuels and Robinson both intend to send their children to public middle schools in the very near future. Although Samuels believes that her biracial child may encounter negative circumstances at a public middle school primarily as the result of exposure to "neighborhood kids," she also stresses that families need to be cautious and investigative in choosing any school for their children, regardless of whether that school is public or private. Because many parents are not able to take the necessary time, even in selecting private schools, they could fall victim to the gimmicks that some MPCP schools devise to bring children into a school that may not have a sound academic program.

Nevertheless, Samuels believes that the MPCP will compel public schools to do a better job, even though current evidence she cites leads her to the conclusion that Milwaukee Public Schools seems to be reacting in a manner that is protective of its overall market position, but not necessarily beneficial to children and their families.

The parents of Marcus Garvey Academy—Shirley Munson, Patrice King, and Ella Mosley—shared in the consensus of the other families regarding the importance of small class sizes within the context of a small-school atmosphere. Based on their experiences, all three parents also stressed that a private school is not necessarily a good school, and a public school is not necessarily a bad school. All three had encountered circumstances in which public schools were the best choice for one or more of their children at a particular time. King and Munson expressed interest in enrolling their children at specific public schools in the future, although Munson realizes that her children would be excluded from the magnet schools she would choose because of their selective admissions policies (in effect making these public schools more private than many private schools).

King and Munson also expressed sympathy for overwhelmed public (and private) school teachers struggling to facilitate learning in overcrowded classroom environments. Nevertheless, both refused to resign their children to chaotic classrooms that would negatively influence them. Rather than offering quality learning experiences, public schools to which they actually have access are, according to one parent, essentially dumping grounds. Such schools are also prone to disciplinary practices that are not oriented to students' or their parents' best interests, and which tend to keep parents "out of the loop" until a problem has erupted to a crisis level.

In contrast, through a school such as Marcus Garvey Academy, the three parents reported that they watched their children progress academically and in matters of self-esteem, as qualities that were previously framed as pathology were recast as strengths.

Toward a Progressive Modernization of Educational Reform Movements

Families in this study who utilize vouchers are therefore relatively unified in their assessment of the qualities that lead them to reject certain schools while choosing others. For many working-class and poor families of color in Milwaukee, vouchers enable their children to escape schools beset by racially pathologizing discourses and overcrowded classrooms. Utilizing vouchers, parents and guardians are able to choose small schools with smaller class sizes, which they believe offer the individualized attention, differentiated curriculum, and situated disciplinary practices that best serve their children. In part, school practices such as these succeed, many parents explained, because the flexibility that private schools can exercise enables them to root such educational practices within the culture, everyday lives, and social conditions of the families they serve.

Although family members interviewed for this study occasionally touched upon neoliberal and neoconservative educational and social themes, I want to suggest that the curricular and pedagogical forms that the interviewed parents and guardians endorsed fit more comfortably alongside a critical and progressive educational agenda than they do within neoliberal and neoconservative scholastic forms. By and large, those interviewed faulted public schools for their universalizing curricula and disciplinary systems, which failed to view students as situated beings with diverse educational needs and preferred learning modalities. Not only did parents and guardians demand curricula, teaching methods, and disciplinary strategies more rooted in students' lives, but a few even pointed out the deeply raced and harmful effects of inappropriately locating African American children and their families within culturally, psychologically, and mentally pathological discursive spaces. This resulted, as some parents and guardians explained to me, from teachers and school officials uncritically appropriating normative frames from middle-class and White contexts of privilege into situations of urban poverty and inequality. As a result of such misappropriation, teachers misconstrued the very dynamics that they believed their interpretive tools and normative frames helped them to understand. Rather than helping students, often despite good intentions, such teachers actually inflicted considerable harm.

Importantly, what caused schools that voucher families rejected to be so out of touch with their students' lived experiences, beyond the presence of privileged teachers unprepared to correctly "read" their less-privileged students' families, was not primarily their inefficiency or even their unresponsiveness (although unresponsiveness was a significant theme). Rather, poor school–family "fit" was largely blamed by those interviewed on overcrowded classrooms, overburdened teachers, and under-resourced schools that were too geographically and culturally distant from where families "lived." For many of those interviewed, that which prevented more manageable classroom sizes and more constructive, culturally appropriate home–school relationships was for the most part a shortage of financial and cultural resources. Public schools serving Milwaukee's working-class and poor families remained inadequately and inequitably funded at the same time that their classrooms were inhabited by teachers who were not sufficiently prepared by teacher education programs to work with students and families whose lives were not as anchored by privilege and mobility as were those of most teacher candidates. Vouchers served as a partial solution for many Milwaukee families because they represented a redistribution of material and symbolic resources to those who did not already possess sufficient amounts of these. With vouchers, families were enabled to select school environments that were perceived to more adequately fit families' real life circumstances and cultural systems of meaning.

Oddly, given the ideological uses most neoliberals and neoconservatives derive from Milwaukee's voucher experiment as an allegedly successful model of educational marketization, the move to vouchers is viewed by many families not as the delivery of a market panacea for failing over-bureaucratized public schools, but rather as a state-sponsored redistributive mechanism that mitigates some of the unfair educational advantages accruing to more privileged families. In this sense, parents, guardians, and community leaders view vouchers as a means for engaging in twin struggles for class and racial justice. At the same time that vouchers are seen as a desirable redistributive form, they are also perceived as enabling a greater degree of community control of schools by marginalized populations. That is, the way that families inhabit the discourses and opportunities of the voucher program seems to coincide more closely, ideologically speaking, with welfarist readings of a state's responsibility to its citizens, as well as to visions of cultural and educational self-determination on the part of marginalized urban communities of color, than it does to models of atomized individuals rationally consuming educational products and thereby bringing efficiency to an educational free market.

Although the way in which families inhabit the voucher program seems to be much more about the politics of redistribution and recognition than it is about markets, efficiency, universal cultural values, and consumerism, nevertheless such neoconservative and neoliberal themes do appear within parents' and guardians' narratives. For example, several interview subjects called for the reform of teachers unions, which were seen to be narrowly self-interested and protective of ineffective, destructive, and even racist teachers and other educational professionals. Furthermore, a few parents stated that administrators should be given greater flexibility in hiring, redirecting, disciplining, and firing teachers as a means for ensuring that teaching practices harmonized more closely with the overall mission of particular community-embedded schools. Even the need for public schools increasingly to compete for their clientele was cited as a positive systemic effect of the creation of the MPCP. These parents saw competition as a means for increasing the responsiveness of Milwaukee Public

Schools to the communities that they served. (Although the argument was also made that competition would actually decrease responsiveness as a school's priorities switched from addressing the needs of its differently situated students to acquiring a more competitive image on a playing field unfairly slanted in favor of more privileged schools.)

Neoconservative themes also sporadically appeared in the narratives of those interviewed. More than one parent implied that poor educational results in public schools were at least in part due to what were seen as parental deficiencies rooted in supposedly pathological Black cultural forms. Related calls for disciplinary law and order, a hallmark of neoconservative educational ideology, were quite apparent in a number of parents' narratives.

Nevertheless, it would be a mistake to simply read these parents' and guardians' invocations of neoliberal and neoconservative themes as evidence of the presence of unmediated neoliberal and neoconservative ideology. A more careful reading actually marks these as discursive reappropriations back into frameworks rooted in collective struggles over redistribution and recognition along lines of race (and class).

I have already mentioned the ways in which vouchers are seen to be less a market solution than a form of state redistributive justice allowing a greater degree of cultural autonomy and educational self-determination. In addition to this, the ways in which neoliberal and neoconservative discourses are inhabited marks them not so much as serving the needs and interests of atomized and individuated consumers, but rather as benefiting marginalized communities as entities organized around racial and socioeconomic solidarity. That is, whereas discourses such as neoliberalism frame their subjects as atomized individuals, the response of Milwaukee's communities of color is often to occupy these subject positions as members of social movements. Just as neoliberals and neoconservatives have sought to appropriate multicultural critiques of bureaucracy into the discourses (and promotional images) surrounding vouchers as a market-based educational form, so too those who use vouchers and the discourses that surround them have attempted to reappropriate neoliberal and neoconservative themes back into more culturally proximate discourses, including calls for social and racial justice, and cultural self-determination.

Further evidence of this reappropriation is present in the way that parents and guardians racially code various interested parties within the voucher debate. Whereas neoliberals frame teachers unions as narrowly self-protective, and educational bureaucracies as inefficient and lacking in market discipline, voucher families suture these critiques back into broader critiques predicated around race and class inequality. Consider the following quote by an African American parent participating in a workshop on parental involvement at the 2001 BAEO symposium in Milwaukee:

> I had two children in private schools. And when I was there initially, my daughter … in kindergarten, I went … and I was in the classroom, I was stopping by, and built that all the way up until middle school. Asked the head of the lower school, can I come in and meet [the teacher]? I want to talk to you about Chelsea … how she's doing, what's going on. And every teacher knew me. And then at the beginning of this year, when she started [public] middle school, I called. And emailed and said, you may know me … I'm Chelsea [last name]'s mother, and I'd like to come in and talk to you about Chelsea and where she's going. "Why don't we wait until we get the first report?" I said, "No, I don't want to wait. I know where Chelsea is. I know how Chelsea is. I know what her ability … I know what she's capable of doing. I know what she does. I want to know who *you* are." (audio transcription of 2001 BAEO symposium workshop)

As is partially illustrated in this parent's narrative, teachers unions and school bureaucracies are positioned as a threat and as discursively White. Meanwhile, independent private schools and the families that populate them are positioned by many voucher families as Black. That is, even for parents and guardians who invoke neoliberal and neoconservative themes, independent private schools and the families that subscribe to them are not primarily exemplars of rational and efficient educational producers and consumers. Rather, in the case of voucher-accepting independent community schools, producers and consumers, artificially split apart from each other within the analytical categories of neoliberal discourse, are reunited within the discourses of pro-voucher families and community leaders as exemplars of, and participants in, racial solidarity. This is why individuals like Mikel Holt are comprehensible when they refer to market-embedded forms of school choice as the "unfinished business of the civil rights struggle" (Holt, 2000). School choice, in the eyes of parents like Dasha Dapedako and Sonia Israel, has become a means to combat White privilege and cultural domination, and bring schools "back to the community" both literally and figuratively.

In sum, teachers unions and educational bureaucracies are not [just] bloated, inefficient, and outdated welfarist forms. They are also neocolonial manifestations of self-serving White cultural institutions that hold the children of urban working-class and poor Black families captive.

Although neoliberal and neoconservative discourses are inhabited and appropriated in creative ways by many Black families and community leaders, it would be romantic and naïve to think that subaltern moves on a terribly uneven playing field, whether individual or collective, would represent a sustainable and long-term strategy for race- and class-based struggles for social justice.

At the same time that we should celebrate the creativity of voucher families who "poach" the subject positions of neoliberal discourses—such as "taxpayer" and "consumer"—in order to fend off the pathological race discourses and poor educational environments within which the "educational establishment" sometimes attempts to confine them, we must also recognize that these tactical moves produce side effects and contain limitations that can be highly undesirable, and which attest to the need for other, more comprehensive, strategies. (For example, tactically inhabiting the subject position of "taxpayer" has the possibly unintended consequence of reinscribing a binary between the deserving/working poor and the non-deserving/unemployed poor, which may actually serve to undermine the educational agenda of those who engage in such "poaching.")

Although the ability of urban Blacks to lay claim to the identities of, and be recognized as, "consumers" and "taxpayers" is itself a testament to the success of decades of anti-racist struggle by people of color and their allies, nevertheless a truly hopeful vision would extend beyond this and enable us to imagine significantly more promising rearticulations of marginalized urban parents and students into ultimately more effective and democratic educational social movements.

That such a rearticulation is not impossible is already evidenced in the aforementioned "closer fit" between the educational needs and desires expressed by the voucher families in this study, on the one hand, and critical, progressive, and multicultural agendas in education, on the other. It is further instantiated in both the tensions that exist among Black voucher advocates and other conservative supporters and in the overlaps that are present between Black urban voucher supporters and their more "traditional" allies—Black civil rights organizations, teachers unions, and civil liberties groups. All of us need to remember that organizations like BAEO will always feel an affinity with groups like the NAACP and the Urban League that is not reciprocated in their relationships with right-wing organizations. That this is the case was confirmed to me in my interviews with BAEO's former executive director Kaleem Caire, who also expressed that he could imagine the sutures that both already exist and that could be further sewn between BAEO and teachers unions such as the NEA over common visions concerning forms of "school choice," such as the more progressive and multicultural instantiations of charter schools, as well as the more responsive relationships with a community's families that are enabled by forms of public school choice.

However, in order for such rearticulations and new alliances to be built, entities like teachers unions and teacher education programs need to be more prepared to discern the "elements of good sense" that do in fact implicate the former in the movement of many urban Black families to conservative educational reforms such as publicly financed private school vouchers. Teachers unions, especially given their implication in, and even participation in, actions that have been deeply neglectful of the best interests of many working-class and poor urban youths of color, must redeem themselves with marginalized populations by clearly and publicly demonstrating an abandonment of narrowly self-interested pursuits and a recommitment to the educational, social, and cultural interests of urban working-class and poor families of color. To the extent that teachers unions have involved themselves in calls for zero tolerance policies as a means to improve teachers' working conditions, and to the extent that unions have been used as a means to protect incompetent, unresponsive, destructive, and racist teachers and other educational professionals, these unions must be reformed.

Furthermore, educational bureaucracies must become significantly more responsive to the needs of the marginalized urban communities that they serve. The ways in which educational bureaucracies have often done the exact opposite has actually helped prepare the ground in places like Milwaukee for the articulations that have been formed between marginalized urban communities and right-wing educational movements, as Milwaukee's sad history of desegregation, organized around what were perceived to be the best educational interests of Milwaukee's privileged White families, aptly demonstrates (Carl, 1995; Fuller, 1985).

Finally, teacher education institutions need to cultivate teacher candidates who are more willing and able to see the families and students with whom they interact in urban school settings (and elsewhere) as situated beings whose lives and experiences are shaped in part by conditions and circumstances that are vastly different from the lived experiences of the

White and middle-class students with whom many teacher candidates feel they can more easily identify. In order to denaturalize the White middle-class normative lens through which all too many teachers view their students' lives, teacher education programs must not only constantly work to de-center whiteness and concomitant class discourses of privilege, but also find new and creative ways to recruit and maintain the enrollment of teacher candidates from less privileged backgrounds.

Although the empirical and conceptual work conducted in this volume provides critical educators with new understandings of the significance of participation among the marginalized in conservative educational reform—and therefore assists us in building more meaningful and effective urban educational reform movements—this volume also has significant theoretical implications.

We can no longer assume that the subaltern simply "become Right" in the process of conservative educational formation. The forms of agency that parents and guardians in this study possess and materialize frequently demonstrate a creative "inhabiting" of the very educational structures and discourses that would seemingly contain and further marginalize them. That is, a discussion of the discourses and subject positions that are "on offer" by various social movements and institutionalized educational forms only tells us part of the story. Such subject positions are not simply offered—they are also inhabited. And it is this latter part of the formulation of identities that has been inadequately theorized and sometimes even neglected within critical education theory.

Stuart Hall has accomplished much in helping critical theorists become more aware of this conceptual "blind spot." In essence, he argues, a successful construction of a theory of identity that is simultaneously non-essentializing yet politically possibilitarian has remained elusive. Current attempts at this project

> offer us a formal account of the construction of subject positions within discourse while revealing little about why it is that certain individuals occupy some subject positions rather than others. ... Discursive subject positions become *a priori* categories which individuals seem to occupy in an unproblematic fashion. (Hall & Du Gay, 1996, p. 10)

He continues (and I quote him here at length, finding his thoughts immensely relevant to the tensions around identity formation explored in this chapter):

What I think we can see [in one of the seminal works on identity cited by critical and post-structural theorists—*Discipline and Punish*] is Foucault being pushed, by the scrupulous rigour of his own thinking, through a series of conceptual shifts at different stages in his work, towards a recognition that, since the decentring of the subject is not the destruction of the subject, and since the "centring" of discursive practice cannot work without the constitution of subjects, the theoretical work cannot be fully accomplished without complementing the account of discursive and disciplinary regulation with an account of the practices of subjective self-constitution. It has never been enough—in Marx, in Althusser, in Foucault—to elaborate a theory of how individuals are summoned into place in the discursive structures. It has always, also, required an account of how subjects are constituted; and in this work, Foucault has gone a considerable way in showing this, in reference to historically-specific discursive practices, normative self-regulation, and technologies of the self. The question which remains is whether we also require to, as it were, close the gap between the two: that is to say, a theory of what the mechanisms are by which individuals as subjects identify (or do not identify) with the "positions" to which they are summoned; as well as how they fashion, stylize, produce and "perform" these positions, and why they never do so completely, for once and all time, and some never do, or are in a constant, agonistic process of struggling with, resisting, negotiating and accommodating the normative or regulative rules with which they confront and regulate themselves. (pp. 13–14)

Hall faults critical and post-structural theories of identity for deferring the question of how the subject is constituted. That is, the subject is "hailed" and interpellated through discourse, through the limited number of subject positions that are on offer, and by the constraints embedded in each—but what is it in the subject that allows it to be hailed in the first place? For Hall, this question is only likely to be advanced "when both the necessity and the 'impossibility' of identities, and the suturing of the psychic and the discursive in their constitution, are fully and unambiguously acknowledged" (Hall & Du Gay, 1996, p. 16).

Although a comprehensive and satisfactory response to Hall's concerns lies well beyond the purview of this volume—not to mention the intellectual capabilities of this author—I want to suggest that the empirical and conceptual work conducted in this volume points to both the necessity and the possibility of a more adequate theorization of this "latter part" of identity formation. Clearly, pro-voucher African American parents, guardians, and community leaders, to again use Hall's words, do not occupy offered subject positions "in an unproblematic fashion." As I argued earlier, and as my empirical work helps demonstrate, parents, guardians, and community leaders adopt, resist, and/or mediate these subject positions in complex, contradictory, and creative ways. These discursive "performances" are products of a subaltern agency which, although perhaps also psychoanalytically derived, is clearly rooted in and formed through the raced, classed, and gendered collective and individual experiences and struggles of working-class and poor African American women and men. That is, identities offered through educational discourses and structures are offered not to blank and amorphous subjects-in-waiting.

Rather than penetrating and constituting an agent-space that is waiting to be "filled up" and completed through discourse—an embryonic agent-space characterized by the "not-yet" and symbolized by a *lack*—conservative educational discourses and their concomitant structural forms instead offer subject positions to identities that are already both richly formed and in formation. These identities, formed and in formation, which are the shifting ground upon which conservative educational discourses must seek to become rooted, are themselves the product of individual and collective histories and struggles. That is, within the process of conservative modernization, conservative educational discursive and structural formations come up against, within an atmosphere of great discursive tension, identities that are already immersed within a constant agonistic process of struggling with, resisting, and negotiating the multiple and contradictory normative discourses with which these latter identities engage themselves. In Milwaukee, the genealogy of this agonistic process of agency and identity has included the decades of raced, classed, and gendered struggle over issues of educational access and self-determination among the city's communities of color, as well as related struggles within other relatively autonomous political, cultural, and economic spheres (McCarthy & Apple, 1988).

In a certain sense, it must be admitted, my retheorization of subaltern agency and identity formation within the process of conservative modernization leaves something to be desired, in that it replicates some of the very weaknesses of which Hall complained. Subaltern agency in conservative formation is theorized in my reformulation as deriving from previous iterations of subaltern processes of agency and identity formation; the question of the constitution of a de-essentialized and discursively constituted subaltern identity and agency is deferred to previous iterations of subaltern processes.

Nevertheless, consciousness of the possible deficiencies within a theory of subaltern processes of identity in conservative formation does not imply the dissolution of this agency. Following Hall, I want to acknowledge "both the necessity and the 'impossibility' of [such] identities" (Hall & Du Gay, p. 16).

Significantly, to postulate subaltern identity processes as both necessary and "impossible" is not to essentialize them. As this volume has argued, subaltern identities do not "naturally" fit into either conservative or radically democratic educational forms and discourses. Nor are such forms and discourses ever simply imposed upon the subaltern. Along with Ernesto Laclau and Chantal Mouffe, I want to emphasize the necessity of reworking Gramscian and other neo-Marxist conceptualizations of the social, so as to remove what these theorists have called the "epistemological obstacles" to the full realization of neo-Marxism's radical political and theoretical potential (Laclau & Mouffe, 1985). They write:

> It is only when the open, unsutured character of the social is fully accepted, when the essentialism of the totality and of the elements is rejected, that this potential becomes clearly visible and "hegemony" can come to constitute a fundamental tool for political analysis on the left. These conditions arise originally in the field of what we have termed the "democratic revolution", but they are only maximized in all their deconstructive effects in the project for a radical democracy, or, in other words, in a form of politics which is founded not upon dogmatic postulation of any "essence of the social", but, on the contrary, on affirmation of the contingency and ambiguity of every "essence", and on the constitutive character of social division and antagonism. (pp. 192–193)

In this volume, Laclau and Mouffe's "unsutured character of the social" is realized in a refusal to ensnare the agency of Black voucher advocates within a paternalistic binary of "false consciousness," on the one hand, and its transcendence through Black realization of the "correctness" of an anti-voucher stance, on the other. Although aspects of his work are highly problematic, I have borrowed in this volume from the work of Michele de Certeau to approach the concerns that surface in the work of Hall, Du Gay, Laclau, and Mouffe. Using conceptual tools appropriated from de Certeau, I have engaged in a retheorization of the agency parents, guardians, and community leaders exercise as they tactically navigate a complex educational terrain that is not largely of their own choosing. That is, although de Certeau's theory of power has the problem of positing strict binaries between essential categories such as "weak" and "strong" and "tactics" and "strategy," and although his theory of power is uniaxial, ahistorical, and essentially immune to transformative collective counter-hegemonic struggle, nevertheless he offers a notion of subaltern agency that has the advantages of being discursively produced, nonessential in regard to "the social," yet cast within relations of power (de Certeau, 1984). Although he is still unable to account for how a "hailed" subject is constituted as a desiring yet nonessential agent, de Certeau's exploration of the manner in which fluid and ephemeral identities are tactically asserted and performed has been quite useful in this research project.

It is my hope that understanding the acts of pro-voucher Black working-class and poor families in this way builds upon Apple and Oliver's crucial work in helping critical educators envision strategies for rearticulating these families' educational concerns to ultimately more effective, meaningful, and democratic educational reform. Hopefully the conceptual modifications that the evidence, such as the interviews with voucher parents and guardians, suggests will assist researchers in other contexts in discerning similar subaltern processes and trajectories and their centrality to processes of conservative modernization. We can imagine that tactical investments in fleeting conservative alliances and subject positions among marginalized communities will play an increasingly significant role both in the United States and elsewhere.

In closing, I want to turn to some of the remaining questions that have been raised but only partially answered in this volume. Although most of these were raised explicitly, there is one lingering question that is implicit in this research, and which must now be answered: Is the particular intersection of race, class, education, and power in Milwaukee so unique that it doesn't tell us much about other urban educational contexts in the United States and elsewhere? Clearly, it must be admitted, Milwaukee does possess fairly unique historical, political, and economic qualities that contributed to its placement at the center of debates, now global in scope, about the character, form, and funding of education. Yet the dynamics of political formation that I have discerned and outlined in this volume—in particular those related to subaltern processes of agency and identity formation—are very likely to appear in other empirical contexts, educational and otherwise, in which the marginalized tactically participate in tenuous alliances with "strange bedfellows" in order to attempt to mitigate some of the worst effects of their marginalization.

The other remaining questions that I have identified were raised more explicitly. I asked the following questions: Have voucher parents been able to get some of the things they desired educationally from articulations with conservative educational forms and discourses? Do progressives have the resources—materially, politically, and culturally—to actualize an agenda that would more effectively meet voucher parents' needs and interests? What is better in the long run for urban working-class and poor families of color—disarticulating their agenda from that of conservatives, or leaving the articulation intact?

I want to propose that, although voucher reforms in Milwaukee have occasionally led to a greater sense of control among urban communities of color over educational resources and agendas, they have not brought about a significant equalization of educational resources and concomitant quality between poor and working-class youths of color and their White and more affluent counterparts in America's suburbs. As Benveniste, Carnoy, and Rothstein have recently argued, the significant division in American educational experiences is not between public and private schools, but rather between urban and suburban schools (Benveniste, Carnoy, & Rothstein, 2003). Urban schools, whether public or private, are massively impacted by inequalities of access to financial and other resources relative to private and public schools serving suburban populations. To the extent that vouchers signal a de-responsibilization of the state in educational matters, they threaten the potential for future processes of equalization.

Nevertheless, I feel progressives and other critical educators, including teachers unions, are committing a grave tactical error when they attempt to erode the partial victories that urban communities of color have actually won in the guise of targeted voucher programs. Such attacks only augment the Right's success in disarticulating traditional alliances forged between teachers unions, other progressive groups, and embattled communities of color. Rather than attempting to "roll back" the MPCP, critical educators should focus on containing its expansion to more privileged communities. In this action, they would presumably be acting in solidarity with most constituencies of color that have favored targeted voucher programs. At the same time, critical educators should work to expose the limitations of voucher reforms, which only partially meet urban parents' needs.

In the present moment, critical educators and other progressives, and their potential and actual urban allies of color, do not possess the material, political, and symbolic resources to actualize an ultimately more meaningful, effective, and democratic educational vision. However, in the long term, articulations among these groups can be "modernized" as a starting point for building new progressive educational social movements. As with the current "modernization" presently in ascendance, the sutures of a *progressive modernization* are sewn only through decades of persistent and committed educational work. Hopefully we will sew with less clumsy and more caring fingers than those we oppose.

APPENDIX

RE-EMBODYING THE
DISEMBODIED RESEARCHER:
NOTES ON METHOD

My name is Tom Pedroni, and I'm currently a graduate student at the University of Wisconsin in Madison. Previous to that I was a public school teacher and a parochial school teacher. I was a public school teacher in New Orleans, Louisiana. And I can attest first hand to a lot of the sentiment that I hear while coming to a symposium like this one by BAEO. It was a school that, I'll be honest—I would never send my children to. No way. Even though there were a lot of committed teachers there. As a public school teacher I taught one hour ... I was a floating teacher. I taught one hour in the boys' locker room. I taught one hour in the small gasoline engines vocational room where I was teaching Civics, and where kids had stuff on their desks that was related to engines, because it hadn't been cleared away from before. And there would be fumes in the air, and a lot of my kids had asthma. So I ... there's no way, if I had any choice, that I would send my kids to a school that was like this.

The author, at the 2002 Symposium of the Black Alliance
for Educational Options

Perhaps a significant number of our scholarly projects are more autobiographical than many of us would care to reveal. I open this appendix on methods with the first few sentences of my intervention as an observer and researcher at the second annual symposium of the Black Alliance of Educational Options in Philadelphia as a way of owning up to the emotional and professional pain that has partially structured my attraction to this topic. To a certain extent, I chose to pursue a study on African American articulation to vouchers in Milwaukee as a way of continuing to work through and come to a better understanding of my own frustration and despair as a teacher of poor and working-class young African American men and women at a public high school in downtown New Orleans.

This is not to say that a project like this is simply therapeutic. My decision to teach in a predominantly African American school was in fact rooted in my own sense that the experience of schooling for Black adolescents in the United States is deeply structured by many of the same material and discursive inequalities that shape American life as a whole. I viewed teaching and learning as deeply political acts, and sought to overcome the anomie and alienation that most of my students felt toward school by making the methods and curriculum of my classroom as relevant to their own everyday lives and interests as possible. In this sense, the despair with which I have wrestled is political. As I learned while teaching, many teachers, perhaps wisely, insulate themselves from this deep sense of grief by retreating from an ethical commitment to their profession and, most significantly, to their students. Although this self-protective anesthetization is not apolitical, it is a way of divesting oneself of the grating everyday struggles from which most urban students of color cannot and do not escape.

On the outside wall of the front of our school building, someone had spray-painted in large curly black lettering, "Intifada USA!" These two simple words actually speak quite eloquently to the educational and social reality many marginalized families in places like New Orleans face. By government provision, students spend their days in a dilapidated and dark building with broken desks. Double fire doors to the outside world remain padlocked with heavy steel chains through the entire school day. There is no gym, and there is no music program. Restrooms contain no doors on the stalls, no toilet paper, and no soap. Teachers are able to make 100 copies a month on the photocopier, assuming they provide their own paper. Unfortunately, the photocopier is often broken. Therefore, teachers who wish to give assignments on paper, or tests, or study guides, must first consult their bank account balances to see if they can afford this. Students are crowded, oftentimes 34 or 37 of them, into a single classroom. As a teacher, I ended up buying eight desks for the classroom into which I floated during fourth period so that my students wouldn't need to sit on the floor any longer. It was bad enough that two of the windows in the classroom were broken.

In short, students at my school in New Orleans were being ware-housed, sometimes even despite the Herculean efforts that many teach-ers, including myself, exerted to make life in school more bearable and more meaningful. But the way that everyday life both inside and outside the classroom wore on my students was in clear evidence. James, one of my homeroom students, in addition to being exceptionally bright, also had a propensity to lash out violently in ways that were even outside the parameters of what might be considered more "normal" violence. That is, fights between boys or between girls were fairly routine, but James would lash out violently and suddenly at people to whom he had little or no con-nection. One day just after the final bell James inexplicably approached a young woman he hardly knew who was exiting from my classroom and punched her harshly and viciously in the side of the face. Besides being injured, the young woman was deeply troubled by the fact that this action against her seemed so random and unpredictable. James was suspended after this incident, and shortly afterward was expelled when he committed further acts of violence.

Several weeks after his expulsion I received some paperwork from a school administrator. James had stabbed his guardian to death with a knife—a woman who was well known in the community for taking in young Black children, particularly young men, who no longer had families to whom they could turn. James lived with her because, when he was five years old, his father had called him on the phone to tell him he was going to kill himself. The phone conversation ended with the sound of a firearm firing. James' mother's whereabouts were not known.

Apparently, soon after James had been expelled from our school, his guardian had threatened to evict him, on the grounds that he was not working hard enough to be responsible. James retaliated. Now the school was requesting that I fill in paperwork that could be used to show a pattern of violent behavior. This would enable him to be tried as an adult, in a state that has the death penalty. I promptly threw the paperwork in the trash.

James' story could be put beside countless others—the cordial and likeable young woman in my ninth grade homeroom who was pregnant with her second child, and who one day seemingly like any other removed three knives from her bag. Or the identical twin of a street level drug dealer and gang leader, who, although occasionally mistaken by the police for his brother, diligently showed up on his own volition several afternoons a week to be tutored by me. Sometimes blades of grass even grow through concrete that is poured on top of them.

But things grow better in rich soil than they do from under concrete, and so when I learned about the creation of a voucher program in Milwaukee, I felt like I could identify with the plight of families who utilized vouchers to free their children from schools that, I imagined, must have shared some qualities with "my" school in New Orleans. Returning to graduate school after a few years of teaching, and encountering already in my first semester seminar debates in which students argued about the harm voucher programs were likely to bring to the very populations they were ostensibly designed to serve, I thought back again to the parents and guardians of students in New Orleans whom I had met. Certainly many of them would have utilized vouchers to pull their children from public school. The viewpoints of one African American doctoral student in particular, in a seminar entitled Ideology and Curriculum, made a significant impact upon me. His reading of vouchers was divergent from almost every other seminar participant, in part because he spoke from the point of view of families in Milwaukee who were utilizing vouchers. He argued that Black families didn't have the time to wait for progressive educational reforms to improve urban education five or ten years down the road—their children's lives were going down the tubes right now.

As a result of these debates, and their confluence with my experiences as a teacher in New Orleans, my seminar papers and research interests began to coalesce around an investigation of the agency of community leaders and marginalized families who utilized vouchers to escape blighted public schools. Within a few weeks, I had made my first contact with Black activists involved in voucher advocacy in Milwaukee.

Access

Kaleem Caire, the Madison-based executive director of the Black Alliance for Educational Options, became my original contact and point of entry into the organizational community around vouchers in Milwaukee. I had become familiar with Caire from reading his interventions on a local electronic mailing list devoted to issues of concern to communities of color. An extensive and heated debate was taking place on the list over the politics of school choice in Madison, Milwaukee, and the United States. Caire's was one of the most articulate voices within the discussion, and his arguments concerning the potential of voucher programs to serve marginalized urban families led me to further question my own beliefs about vouchers and the strategic wisdom of African American advocates for educational marketization. Because Caire lived in Madison until June 2001, I was able to contact him on the phone to ask him further questions about various assertions he had made on the electronic mailing list. In our first discussion, Caire graciously invited me to observe the BAEO's first national symposium taking place in Milwaukee the following week.

Caire's openness to someone so unknown to him needs to be noted. Because of my association with some of the primary "Left" opponents of educational privatization, including Michael Apple and Alex Molnar, Caire knew that I was very likely to be a voucher opponent. My initial phone conversations with Caire were a delicate walk between wanting to be frank and honest about my dispositions toward vouchers, and wanting nevertheless to convince him that I had an open mind and could be trusted to research BAEO and the voucher movement in Milwaukee fairly. His invitation to observe the symposium came despite the fact that I was White, that the symposium was intended only for African Americans, and that other prominent individuals in the organization had already become vocal about the need for him to curtail further invitations, particularly of Whites.

Not only did Caire enable my access to the first BAEO symposium and the initial set of field notes this generated for this study, but he also agreed to a subsequent lengthy interview, and pointed me in the direction of future meetings organized by BAEO. In many ways, Caire has been an ideal informant. This quality is probably due in part to the partial overlap of our life worlds. Both Caire and I have worked in schools in the city of Madison. Furthermore, both of us share a keen interest in social justice issues. Finally, Caire and I had both done a fair amount of coursework with individuals like Michael Apple in the Department of Curriculum and Instruction at the University of Wisconsin.

Research Methods of the Study

The fieldwork and analysis conducted for this study were designed to assist us in understanding the ways in which conservative educational mobilizations succeed by appealing to and connecting with the "good sense" and everyday needs and desires of people who would not normally conceive of themselves as conservative educational activists. Discerning the subtle shifts through which parents and guardians align themselves with and participate in such movements would help uncover both the opportunities that progressive educational actors have missed, and the spaces for action that continue to present themselves as a result of the persistence of needs unmet by market-based educational reforms.

In centering my ethnographic fieldwork on instances of parental articulation with the conservative alliance around vouchers in Milwaukee, my hope was that we would be enabled to answer such questions as: How do the discourses that parents and guardians mobilize both coincide with and differ from the discourses of the conservative alliance? How do parents and guardians act within, subvert, or reject the subject positions that are offered them, both by the Right and by the Milwaukee Public Schools "educational establishment"?

Chapter 4 in this volume examined the articulations formed at the macro-level between the BAEO and other, mostly conservative and nationally dominant, groups within the voucher alliance. It also mapped out the articulations formed within BAEO itself, both at a leadership level, and between leadership and the "grassroots," constituted primarily by school administrators, educational activists, and real and potential voucher parents and guardians.

The main sources of data for the macro-analysis in Chapter 4 were interviews conducted with Kaleem Caire, BAEO's executive director in 2001, and Howard Fuller, the founder and chair of BAEO. The analysis in Chapter 4 was also informed by observations and informal interviews at the first three annual symposia of the BAEO.

But my primary sources of field data in addressing the core questions of this research were interviews with sets of parents and guardians at five schools participating in the Milwaukee Parental Choice Program. The majority of the selected parents and guardians were in what we might call a "liminal" space between a previously utilized school—quite often a public school—and a school participating in the voucher program. My purpose in speaking with them was primarily to discern the push and pull factors that guided them in rejecting other school options and choosing the school at which their children are now enrolled. The first (the push factors) would be ones with which we, as progressive educators, would presumably be sympathetic—distressed conditions in urban schools, both materially and in terms of the race and class discourses that permeate them. An analysis of the second set of factors—the pull factors—would help illustrate how parents and families construct private schools as different from those they rejected. What did they see the selected MPCP school offering relative to the rejected school(s)? What is the symbolic or cultural capital that voucher families find circulating through a particular voucher school that they identify as vital to their interests and the interests of their children?

I want to remind my readers at this point that I did not enter into my core research context "raw." As mentioned previously, the methods that I have utilized, and which I describe below, have been theoretically informed by and practically enabled (in terms of access) by my earlier field work concerning the BAEO, as well as by the discursive analyses I conducted of interviews with African American parental supporters of the MPCP in my "pilot" research. Particularly, my participation in and observation of the first three annual BAEO symposia had facilitated my introduction to and familiarity with school administrators and other key players in the Milwaukee vouchers context. My acquaintance with these individuals was crucial in establishing research relationships predicated on a considerable degree of trust with parents, guardians, administrators, and teachers at the various schools in the study. Especially given the very real tensions over issues of race, class, gender, and educational access, along with my positionality as a middle-class, European-American male academic, this access, as well as the trust established in these relationships, has been pivotal to my ability to engage in meaningful research.

At the core of this study, then, is the field research I conducted in and around five private and parochial schools participating in the MPCP. Each of the five schools was selected according to the following two criteria: (1) Does the school have significant voucher enrollment? (2) Does the school approximate one of the five general "mission" categories I discerned in my assessment of the range of MPCP schools: Catholic, non-Catholic religious, Afro-centric, independent, and "at risk"-oriented.

In order to locate five suitable schools for inclusion in the study, I consulted the website of the Wisconsin Department of Public Instruction, where I found listings of all schools participating in the MPCP. I categorized all of these schools according to their basic mission, assessed the percentage of students in each who used a voucher to attend, and examined the schools' racial, linguistic, and cultural composition. Not only did

I want to choose five schools that were representative of each of the five broad categories, but I also wanted the schools to represent a "balance" of other attributes. For example, I wanted to include both high schools and K4–8 and/or K4–5 schools. I also wanted to include at least one single-sex school. I wanted the schools to be fairly dispersed throughout the City of Milwaukee. Furthermore, I wanted to choose schools that were representative, in the best estimation I could make, of both some of the "best" and the "worst" the program had to offer. That is, I wanted to be sure to include some of the "flagship" schools of the program. However, recognizing that the five or six schools that most typically receive attention in the press and in documentaries only enroll about 10% of children participating in the MPCP, I wanted to be sure to also include schools that were less well-known and which oftentimes, at least initially, seemed less exemplary.

To discern which schools were the "flagship" schools, I consulted a variety of newspaper articles about schools in the program, and inquired of Kaleem Caire his sense of which schools were most commonly heralded as exemplary. This gave me both the most public perspective (from newspapers) as well as a "movement insider" perspective (from Caire) on which schools were commonly celebrated as the most positive representations of the program.

In order to locate what were potentially less "savory" schools, I conducted research on the Web and located newspaper stories that reported alleged or actual legal, ethical, or scholastic misdeeds at the MPCP schools. I also scouted for schools that were simply not mentioned in any reviews, positive or negative, that I encountered.

In the end, although I make no claim to having obtained a scientifically representative sample of the schools, I can assert that the schools I located, contacted to participate, and eventually selected for the study, were indeed a mix of many of the qualities I had been seeking. Not all of the schools I contacted agreed to participate in the study. Two of the eight I contacted "declined" participation by simply not responding to the numerous letters, emails, and phone calls I placed with the schools. One school, which had been highly recommended to me by both Caire and by numerous other BAEO symposium participants, was removed from possible inclusion in the study after the administrator explained that the school's entire board would need to participate in the approval of the study, which would place an undue burden upon the school, and would likely result in refusal of participation in any case. Another school's administrator, who in the end agreed to participate in the study, complained about the overuse to which she felt her school had been subjected by teams of researchers who proved to be much more intrusive and consuming of teaching and work time than had initially been promised.

All five schools that eventually agreed to participate welcomed me with open arms, inviting me to stop in and observe more or less at any time. Interviews were never declined, and considerable effort was expended in order to identify suitable families for participation in the study. During my field observations at the five schools, administrators worked hard to enable me to visit precisely the classrooms and the class periods I had requested to observe. Regardless of whether or not what I saw in the schools was actually impressive or disturbing, I could not detect any attempt on the part of administrators or teachers to shield me from viewing particular aspects of school life, nor did I feel that teachers or administrators were "putting on a show" for an outside researcher. In short, school personnel seemed willing to let me see their schools "warts and all." One principal, when asked what an appropriate pseudonym for her Catholic girls' school might be, offered "Our Lady of the Washing Machine."

It is important to note that my "entrée" to each of the schools was not simply by way of the subject position of "neutral university researcher." Rather, as alluded to earlier, I attempted to form relationships that were as predicated on trust as possible. Instead of contacting schools "cold," I asked Caire to make the initial contact with each school on my behalf in order to explain a bit about my research project, identify who I was as a person, and affirm that I could be trusted to study the school—and particularly a few families of the school—fairly. As I met each administrator, and for that matter each parent or guardian, for the first time, I explained the way in which I was "situated" within the research not only as a Ph.D. student with particular dispositions toward vouchers (which I was quite frank about), but also as a teacher, as a person interested in educational reform, and as a participant observer in the BAEO symposia. I feel that had I instead assumed a less personable and more detached "neutral researcher" posture, the access I would have been granted might have been considerably diminished.

After having chosen one MPCP school to represent each "mission" category as described above, I then sought to identify three newly subscribed families at each school to participate in the study. I asked each school's administrator to consider the following guidelines in nominating and providing contact information for families: (1) to identify one family that was very new to the school, (2) to identify a family that had left the school fairly recently, and (3) to identify a family that was more established within the school. Furthermore, I explained to each administrator that I was specifically interested in the participation of African American families within the MPCP.

Administrators at the five schools followed my requests with varying degrees of adherence to the guidelines I had established. Although all five schools had no difficulty in locating both a new and a more established family to participate in the study, receptivity to helping me locate a family that had recently left the school varied significantly. Whereas the administrator and staff at Mariama Abdullah School bent over backwards to facilitate my access to a parent who had recently withdrawn her children from the school for reasons that remained unknown, another administrator, at Knowledge Ventures Learning Academy, stated frankly that it would not be in his best interest to put me in touch with a recently departed family, since the family would only have negative things to say about the school. The three other schools simply sidestepped my request for a departed parent without comment.

There was also variance in the degree to which administrators complied with my request for African American parents and guardians for the study. Although I had explained that I was specifically interested in the question of African American articulation to voucher reform as part of a decades-long struggle for access to quality education and educational self-determination, two of the parents with whom I was put in contact were not African American.

In all, thirteen of the fifteen parents were African American, one was European American, and one was Latina. It became clear to me only after the interviews that all of the nominated families were coded by the school as Black because all of the children receiving vouchers within these families had African ancestry. One child's parents were a biracial couple. Another had been adopted as a foster child by his Latina mother. It's quite possible that the administrators simply assumed that each of the parents or guardians was also African American.

Fourteen of the fifteen interview subjects were women. How this gender disparity in interview subjects came to be is itself an interesting issue. Most of the schools simply gave me the names of female parents outright. Two gave me the names of both a child's male and female parent, at least in cases where the school possessed both names. Although I did not inquire about the marital or relationship status of each interviewed parent, most volunteered that they were single mothers, and some elaborated that they maintained little or no contact with the children's fathers.

I also do not know how best to interpret the fact that most school administrators gave me the names of female parents only. This may reflect the fact that the school knew some of the women to be single parents, that the female parent had functioned as the primary representative of the family in interactions with the school, or that the school assumed, perhaps for patriarchal reasons, that a female parent would be more available or more appropriate for interviews about a family's children. It may have also reflected a racialized (and problematic) assumption on the part of the school that African American fathers could be assumed to be absent from the lives of their children.

In two out of four cases in which I was given the name of both a male and female parent, it was the female parent who elected to be interviewed. In one case, both the male and female parent came to the interview, but the male parent remained almost entirely silent during the interview, except when questioned directly. In the remaining case, I was put into contact only with the male parent. That this family was going through a separation at the time of this study may have played a role in the fact that both parents were not present for the interview.

Fourteen of the fifteen families spoke English as a first language. My interview with the Latina foster parent was translated "in real time" by her daughter.

Each parent or guardian was interviewed two to three times. First, each parent was contacted by phone so that I could explain the research, and parents could ask any questions they had. During this call I also verified both their willingness to participate in the study, and their appropriateness based on the circumstances of their child's enrollment in the school. Next, each parent or guardian participated in a face to face semi-structured interview which typically lasted 30 minutes to an hour or more.

In each of these interviews, my purpose was to identify how parents and guardians as individuals and as a group occupied the space offered by the voucher reform. How did the voucher reform overlap with their concerns and interests, and how did it fall short? How did MPCP parents and guardians "inhabit" the identities offered to them by neoliberal and neoconservative voucher advocates? Similarly, how did they "inhabit" the discourses of neoliberalism and neoconservatism? Finally, what can be learned from parents and guardians about how poor and working-class voucher families might be rearticulated into a more effective and democratic educational vision?

Questions and themes that were directly addressed in the interviews with parents and guardians typically included the following:

- What do you feel that [selected MPCP school] offers that [rejected school] does not?
- Why do you feel that [selected MPCP school] is able to offer this? What is it about the school that makes it able to offer an education for your child that you are more satisfied with?
- How do you feel about your decision to move your child from [rejected school] to [selected MPCP school]? Are you satisfied?
- How did you find out about the voucher (Milwaukee Parental Choice Program) program?
- What led you to be interested in taking your child out of [rejected school]? What would have to change about [rejected school] to make you comfortable with having your child there?
- What do you feel is the reason for [rejected school] having the problems that it does?
- Do you feel in general that privately run schools are a better idea than publicly run schools? Why?
- Was [selected MPCP school] your first choice? If not, what was the process by which you came to place your child at this school? If it was your first choice, why was this school your first choice?

After the formal semi-structured interviews had been completed and transcribed, I conducted follow-up phone interviews with parents and guardians as needed in order to obtain information that would round out my understanding of the comments they had shared with me in the first two interviews.

The sets of interviews with parents and guardians were supplemented by interviews and observations at their associated schools. First, I interviewed the principal at each of the schools two times. The initial interview was a less formal opportunity for me to explain my research, assess the appropriateness of the school for the study, and begin the process of identifying likely candidates among parents and guardians at the school for inclusion in the study. The second interview with the principal was semi-structured and more formal in format, conducted only after the sets of observations were completed at the respective school. At this second interview, questions centered on the marketing activities of the schools, and the perceived impact of participating in the MPCP on the school's pedagogy, curriculum, and culture. The purpose of the more formal interviews with administrators was primarily to give me a greater sense of the manner in which the school sought to articulate itself with the educational hopes, visions, and concerns of subscribing and potentially subscribing families. Each of the semi-structured interviews lasted 45 to 75 minutes, and typically consisted of questions such as:

- Why did [name of school] decide to participate in the MPCP? What arguments were posed supporting participation? What arguments were posed rejecting participation?
- Why do you think participating MPCP parents have chosen [name of school]? What is it that this school offers to these parents that MPS schools and other private and MPCP schools do not?
- Has the school's participation in the MPCP led to any shifts in mission, curriculum, or pedagogy? If so, why?
- In what type of marketing and promotional activities has [name of school] engaged in order to attract MPCP students and their parents?
- Has there been any student or teacher attrition from the school as a result of its participation in the MPCP?

Finally, I conducted informal interviews and field observations with two to three teachers and their classrooms at each school. The primary purpose of this data collection was to gain a greater sense of the intersection of the "educational product delivered" with parents' and guardians' expectations and demands, as expressed in their interviews. Furthermore, my field experiences at each of the schools assisted me in contextualizing parents' and guardians' interview responses. To maximize this benefit, I sought whenever possible to observe the classrooms and teachers of children whose families participated in the study. Field observations in schools typically lasted one school day, and consisted of visits to anywhere from two to nine classrooms, depending on the particular school context.

The informal interviews with teachers were conducted immediately after classroom observations and centered on teachers' perceptions of

MPCP parents' and guardians' educational desires and concerns, and the ability of the school to meet those concerns.

Each of the more formal, semi-structured interviews with parents, guardians, and principals was audio-recorded, cataloged, fully transcribed, coded, and analyzed. I obtained written and verbal consent from each of the interview participants under the terms outlined in an approved letter of informed consent. Finally, I collected field notes during each of the classroom observations and informal interviews with teachers.

A Final Word of Caution

I want to end this appendix on methods with a word of caution. In presenting the narratives of the parents, guardians, and other individuals with whom I conducted interviews, I want to be sure I have not engaged in what might be called a ruse of authenticity.

That is, I wouldn't want to reproduce the notion, either in my interviews, or in the segments that I have excerpted for this study, that I've simply allowed the respective individuals to "speak for themselves." It would be deeply unethical, and counterproductive to my own purposes and intentions, were I to use the presence of their voices to naturalize and reify my analysis of "their" speech.

Elements of co-construction permeate what is communicated through the interviews and their analysis. First, those who are speaking in the interviews were aware that they were not speaking to a disembodied interviewer or researcher. Rather, they knew that the person with whom they were speaking was embodied and situated within unequal relations of power in particular ways. In a certain sense, especially given the volatile nature of issues like vouchers and unequal access to education, parents and guardians shared their stories with me in a context in which what they communicated could have been used to the great detriment of the individuals involved, either individually, by jeopardizing families' relationships to particular institutions, or collectively, as information could be misused in opportunistic and unethical attacks on the MPCP, in which they as participants have a very real interest. These tensions, risks, and inequalities inevitably impacted the exchanges in this field research.

Beyond the co-construction implied by such dynamics, what I present is "selective" in other ways. In most instances, I guided the conversation, selected which questions were important to ask, and framed the responses that were given. Later, I determined without any particular input from those interviewed which of their instances of speech were "meaningful" enough to be included for analysis in this research. This is not to say the participants were completely without agency in the interviews. Nonetheless, it is an agency constrained by factors such as the ones I have described in this book.

NOTES

Chapter 2

1. In making this critique of the bureau-professional welfare state, as Clarke and Newman point out, the New Right has actually creatively blended its own themes with the themes of many other critics of the old state form. Some of these critiques emanated from the "New Left" and other new social movements, including feminists, environmentalists, and activists of color, who had criticized the social democratic state for its "one size fits all" operating logic.

2. However, Clarke and Newman do not wish to seem reductive by implying that managerialism is seamlessly imposed onto various state institutions. In their empirical research, they find that managerialist discourse is in fact mediated, contested, and creatively misunderstood at every level. Sometimes, as Clarke and Newman show, its logics are reinterpreted into visions and practices that are actually, and not just rhetorically, beneficial to the state's "consumers."

3. Perhaps "weak" is not the most ideal descriptor in this instance. The neoliberal state remains quite "strong" in the policing it undertakes of populations on the social formation's margins, which neoliberal theory marks as expendable. This truth is encountered on a regular basis by those "jettisoned" populations residing in the urban cores of the United States, as well as within burgeoning prisons. As Apple and others have noted, the neoliberal state seeks to privatize the profits generated within current forms of market capitalism, at the same moment that it socializes—through state provision of prisons, for example—the costs of these arrangements (Apple, 1985); for a further discussion of "jettisoned" populations such as prisoners within the neoliberal state, see Pedroni (2001).

4. Apple and Oliver characterize the parents in the textbook controversy as initially having political intuitions that were "not fully formed in any oppositional sense" (Apple, 1996, p. 61). In this chapter I use the phrase "ideologically unformed" or "ideologically relatively unformed" to refer to this quality of parents' ideology as conceptualized by Apple and Oliver. By "unformed" ideology I do not mean "without" ideology. Rather, I am trying to capture Apple and Oliver's sense of their ideology as not (yet) explicitly cohering to a singular ideological stream within conservative thought and conservative discourse in the United States. Their ideology is less "worked out"; they are less overtly politicized, at least initially.

Chapter 3

1. Audiovisual copies of this interview were given to the author directly by the videographer. Complete transcripts of the interview upon which the analysis here is based, as well as copies of the original audiovisual interview, are available from the author upon request.

Chapter 5

1. Readers may notice in the sections that follow, as I discuss parents' and guardians' comments interview by interview, that the length of my discussion from one individual to another varies considerably. This is not a reflection of my privileging of some interview subjects' voices over others. Rather, the variation reflects a variation in depth of response among the different study participants.
2. Learnfare is a component of Wisconsin Works (W-2), the state-created welfare entity formed in Wisconsin at the time that federal legislation under the Welfare Reform Act devolved most aspects of social welfare provision to the 50 states. Under Learnfare, parents who are placed in jobs funded through Wisconsin Works are fined if their school-age children are not enrolled in schools. Learnfare students meet regularly with "Case Managers," who, beyond monitoring enrollment and attendance, provide the following services: "assessment, career development and planning, problem solving and role play, non-traditional counseling, crisis counseling and intervention, supportive services, and referral to community services" (Wisconsin Department of Workforce Development website). Learnfare is a prime example of the devolutionary state's greater involvement in the private domain. As Clarke and Newman argue, "the shift of responsibilities to families has been accompanied by the subjection of households to greater state surveillance, regulation, and intervention" (Clarke & Newman, 1997, p. 28).

REFERENCES

Apple, M. W. (1985). *Education and power*. Boston: Routledge and Kegan Paul, ARK edition.

Apple, M. W. (1993). *Official knowledge: Democratic education in a conservative age*. New York: Routledge.

Apple, M. W. (1996). *Cultural politics and education*. New York: Teachers College Press.

Apple, M. W. (2000). Standards, subject matter, and a romantic past: A review of Left back: A century of failed school reforms by Diane Ravitch. *Educational Policy*, 15(2), 323–334.

Apple, M. W. (2001). *Educating the "right" way: Markets, standards, God, and inequality*. New York: RoutledgeFalmer.

Apple, M. W. (2006). *Educating the "right" way: Markets, standards, God, and inequality* (2nd ed.). New York: Routledge.

Apple, M. W., & Beane, J. A. (Eds.). (2007) *Democratic schools: Lessons in powerful education*, (2nd edition). Portsmouth, NH: Heinemann.

Apple, M. W., & Buras, K. L. (Eds.). (2006). *The subaltern speak: Curriculum, power, and educational struggle*. New York: Routledge.

Apple, M. W., & Oliver, A. (2003). *Becoming right: Education and the formation of conservative movements*. In M.W. Apple, P. Aasen, M. K. Cho, L. A. Gandin, A. Oliver, Y.-K. Sung, et al., *The state and the politics of knowledge*. New York: RoutledgeFalmer.

Apple, M. W. & Pedroni, T. C. (2005). Conservative alliance building and African American support of voucher reforms: The end of Brown's promise or a new beginning? *Teachers College Record*, 107, 2068–2105.

Arnot, M., David, M., & Weiner, G. (1999). *Closing the gender gap: Postwar education and social change*. Cambridge, UK: Polity Press.

Ball, S. (1994). *Education reform: A critical and post-structural approach*. Buckingham, UK: Open University Press.

Bennett, W. (1988). *Our children and our country*. New York: Simon and Schuster.

Benveniste, L., Carnoy, M., & Rothstein, R. (2003). *All else equal: Are public and private schools different?* New York: RoutledgeFalmer.

Black Alliance for Educational Options (BAEO) Website. Retrieved August 11, 2003, from http://www.baeo.org/.

Black Alliance for Educational Options (BAEO). (2001). 2001 Symposium in Milwaukee [Program]. Author.

Black Alliance for Educational Options (BAEO). (2002). 2002 Symposium in Philadelphia [Program]. Author.

Black Alliance for Educational Options (BAEO). (2003). 2003 Symposium in Dallas [Program]. Author.

Black America's Political Action Committee (BAMPAC) Website. Retrieved October 12, 2006, from http://www.bampac.org/bampac_directors.asp.

Bloom, A. (1987). *The closing of the American mind: How higher education has failed democracy and impoverished the souls of today's students.* New York: Simon and Schuster.

Buras, K. L. (1999). Questioning core assumptions: A critical reading of and response to E. D. Hirsch's The schools we need and why we don't have them. *Harvard Educational Review,* 69(1), 67–93.

Carl, J. (1995). *The politics of education in a new key: The 1988 Chicago School Reform Act and the 1990 Milwaukee Parental Choice Program.* Unpublished doctoral dissertation, University of Wisconsin, Madison.

Carl, J. (1996). Unusual allies: Elite and grass-roots origins of parental choice in Milwaukee. *Teachers College Press,* 98, 266–285.

Carr, S. (2003). Lawmakers want wider voucher plan. *Milwaukee State Journal,* April 10, 2003. Retrieved October 12, 2006, from http://www.schoolchoiceinfo.org/news/index.cfm?action=detail&news_id=592.

Chomsky, N. (1999). *Profit over people: Neoliberalism and global order.* New York: Seven Stories Press.

City of Milwaukee Health Department. (2000). Milwaukee childhood lead poisoning prevention program: Facts about childhood lead poisoning. Retrieved August 10, 2003, from http://www.ci.mil.wi.us/citygov/health/lead/facts.htm.

Clarke, J., & Newman, J. (1997). *The managerial state: Power, politics and ideology in the remaking of social welfare.* London: Sage Publications.

CNN.com. (2002). Police: 8 youths confess in Milwaukee death. Retrieved October 12, 2006, from http://www.cnn.com/2002/US/Midwest/10/02/milwaukee.beating/index.html.

Corporation for Educational Radio and Television. (1993). Liberating America's schools [Video]. New York: PBS.

Creative Media Services/CMS (1998). Interview segments. [Video]. Milwaukee: Author.

De Certeau, M. (1984). *The practice of everyday life.* Berkeley, CA: University of California Press.

DelFattore, J. (1992). *What Johnny shouldn't read: Textbook censorship in America.* New Haven, CT: Yale University Press.

Dillard, A. (2001). *Guess who's coming to dinner now?* New York: New York University Press.

D'Souza, D. (1992). *Illiberal education: The politics of race and sex on campus.* New York: Vintage Books.

Dougherty, J. (2004). *More than one struggle: The evolution of Black school reform in Milwaukee.* Chapel Hill, NC: University of North Carolina Press.

Dyson, M. E. (1993). *Reflecting Black: African American cultural criticism.* Minneapolis, MN: University of Minnesota Press.

Fanon, F. (1967). *Black skin, White masks.* New York: Grove Press.

Fraser, N. (1989). *Unruly practices: Power, discourse and gender in contemporary social theory.* Minneapolis, MN: University of Minnesota Press.

Freire, P. (1993). *Pedagogy of the oppressed.* New York: Continuum.

Fuller, H. (1985). *The impact of the Milwaukee Public Schools system's desegregation plan on Black students and the Black community (1976–1982).* Unpublished doctoral dissertation. Marquette University.

Gee, J., Hull, G., & Lankshear, C. (1996). *The new work order.* Sydney: Allen and Unwin.

Ginwright, S. A. (2004). *Black in school: Afrocentric reform, urban youth, and the promise of hip-hop culture.* New York: Teachers College Press.

Glazer, N. (1997). *We are all multiculturalists now.* Cambridge, MA: Harvard University Press.

Gramsci, A. (1971). *Selections from the prison notebooks of Antonio Gramsci.* Trans. Q. Hoaren & G. Smith. New York: International Publishers.

Greene, J. (2001). *High school graduation rates in the United States*. Washington, DC: Black Alliance for Educational Options.

Hall, S., & Du Gay, P. (Eds.), (1996). *Questions of cultural identity*. Thousand Oaks, CA: Sage Publications.

Harvey, D. (1989). *The condition of postmodernity*. Cambridge, MA: Blackwell.

Herrnstein, R., & Murray, C. (1994). *The bell curve*. New York: Free Press.

Hess, F. M., & Finn, C. E. (Eds.) (2004). *Leaving no child behind?* New York: Palgrave.

Hirsch, E. D., Jr. (1996). *The schools we need and why we don't have them*. New York: Anchor Books.

Holt, M. (2000). *Not yet "free at last": The unfinished business of the Civil Rights Movement: Our battle for school choice*. Oakland, CA: Institute for Contemporary Studies.

Institute for the Transformation of Learning (ITL) Website. Retrieved August 10, 2003, from http://www.itlmuonline.com/.

Jones, J. (1985). *Labor of love, labor of sorrow: Black women, work, and the family from slavery to the present*. New York: Vintage Press.

King, J., (Ed.). (2005). *Black education: A transformative research and action agenda for the new century*. Mahwah, NJ: Lawrence Erlbaum Associates.

Kliebard, H. M. (1987). *The struggle for the American curriculum 1893–1958*. New York: Routledge and Kegan Paul.

Laclau, E., & Mouffe, C. (1985). *Hegemony and socialist strategy*. London: Verso.

Lauder, H., & Hughes, D. (1999). *Trading in futures: Why markets in education don't work*. Buckingham: Open University Press.

Major, R., (Ed.). (2001). *Educating our Black children: New directions and radical approaches*. London: Routledge.

Marable, M. & Mullings, L. (Eds). (2000). *Let nobody turn us around: Voices of resistance, reform, and renewal: An African American anthology*. Lanham: Rowman & Littlefield.

McCarthy, C., & Apple, M. W. (1988). Race, class and gender in American educational research: Toward a nonsynchronous parallelist position. *Perspectives in Education*, 4(2), 67–69.

Media Transparency (2003). The Lynde and Harry Bradley Foundation. Retrieved August 10, 2003, from http://www.mediatransparency.org/funders/bradley_foundation.htm.

Meier, D., & Wood, G. (Eds.) (2004). *Many children left behind*. Boston: Beacon Press.

Mitchell, T. (2002, October 23). Emerging "culture of death" starts to grip city in wake of beating death. *Milwaukee Community Journal*, 26(16), pp. 1–3.

Metz, M. (2003). *Different by design*. New York: Teachers College Press.

Miner, B. (1997). Splits widen within Wisconsin voucher movement. *Rethinking Schools*, 11(4).

Molnar, A. (1996). *Giving kids the business: The commercialization of America's schools*. Boulder, CO: Westview Press.

Pedroni, T. C. (2001). *The rise of the managerial state and the decline of rehabilitation in the United States: A conjunctural and discursive analysis of a 1993 "late-rehabilitation" prison education reform proposal in the context of conservative modernization*. Unpublished master's thesis, University of Wisconsin, Madison.

Pedroni, T. C. (2004). State theory and urban school reform II: A reconsideration from Milwaukee. In D. Gabbard & E. W. Ross (Eds.), *Defending public education: Schooling and the rise of the security state* (pp.131–140). New York: Greenwood Publishing.

Pedroni, T. C. (2005). É possível combinar as abordagens pós-estruturalistas e neo-marxistas? A construção de uma abordagem composta na teoria e na pesquisa educacional crítica. *Cadernos de Educação, FaE/UFPel*, Pelotas, 25, pp. 9-31.

People for the American Way (PFAW). (2001). Community voice or captive of the right? A closer look at the Black Alliance for Educational Options. December 2001. Retrieved October 12, 2006, from http://www.pfaw.org/pfaw/dfiles/file_66.pdf.

Peterson, P. E., & West, M. R. (Eds.) (2003). *No child left behind?* Washington, D.C.: Brookings Institution Press.

Public Policy Forum (1999, June 8). Exploring parents' educational options. *In Fact*, 887(6), 1–6.

Ravitch, D. (2000). *Left back: A century of failed school reforms*. New York: Simon and Schuster.

Reed, R. (1994). *After the revolution: How the Christian Coalition is impacting America*. Dallas, TX: Word Publishing.

Rofes, E., & Stulberg, L. M. (Eds.). (2004). *The emancipatory promise of charter schools: Toward a progressive politics of school choice*. Albany, NY: State University of New York Press.

Rury, J. L., & Cassell, F. A. (1993). *Seeds of crisis: Public schooling in Milwaukee since 1920*. Madison, WI: University of Wisconsin Press.

Stedman, L. (1998). An assessment of the contemporary debate over U.S. achievement. In D. Ravitch (Ed.), *Brookings Papers on Educational Policy*: 1998 (53–84). Washington, D.C.: Brookings Institution.

U.S. Census Bureau. (2000). Housing patterns: Residential segregation of Blacks or African Americans: 1980 to 2000. Retrieved October 12, 2006, from http://www. census.gov/hhes/www/housing/resseg/ch5.html.

Valenzuela, A. (Ed.) (2005). *Leaving children behind*. Albany, NY: State University of New York Press.

Wells, A. S., Lopez, A., Scott, J., & Holme, J. (1999). Charter schools as postmodern paradox: Rethinking social stratification in the age of deregulated school choice. *Harvard Educational Review*, 69(2), 172–204.

West, C. (1982). *Prophesy deliverance! An Afro-American revolutionary Christianity*. Philadelphia: Westminster Press.

Whitty, G., Power, S., & Halpin, D. (1998). *Devolution and choice in education: The school, the state, and the market*. Buckingham: Open University Press.

Wisconsin Department of Public Instruction. (1998). Milwaukee Parental Choice Program: Pupil count history, 1990 to present. Retrieved August 10, 2003, from http:// www.dpi.state.wi.us/dpi/dfm/sms/histnum.html.

Wisconsin Department of Public Instruction. (2002a). Milwaukee Parental Choice Program: MPCP facts and figures for 2002-2003. Retrieved August 10, 2003, from http://www.dpi.state.wi.us/dpi/dfm/sms/doc/mpc02fnf.doc.

Wisconsin Department of Public Instruction. (2002b). The Milwaukee Parental Choice Program: Information for parents. Retrieved August 10, 2003, from http://www. dpi.state.wi.us/dpi/dfm/sms/pdf/mpcbro02.pdf.

Wisconsin Department of Workforce Development. (2002). Wisconsin Works (W-2): Learnfare. Retrieved May 6, 2004, from http://www.dwd.state.wi.us/dws/w2/learnfare.htm

Witte, J. (2000). *The market approach in education: An analysis of America's first voucher program*. Princeton, NJ: Princeton University Press.

INDEX